DEFENCE PROGRAMMES OF INDIA

DEFENCE PROGRAMMES OF INDIA

H B Mishra

AUTHORSPRESS
PUBLISHERS OF SCHOLARLY BOOKS

First Published 2000
by Authorspress

Reprinted 2001

E-35/103, Jawahar Park (Shree Ganesh Complex)
Laxmi Nagar, Delhi-110092
e-mail: authorspress@yahoo.com

Typeset in NewCenturySchlbk by Chitra Computers

Defence Programmes of India
ISBN 81-7273-008-X

Printed in India at Tarun Offset, Delhi.

Preface

The defence policy accommodates continuing changes in the strategic setting whilst ensuring that the armed forces deployed are well equipped, properly manned and supported to allow them to undertake operations effectively. It is equally necessary to ensure that they are capable of responding to future challenges. The force structure is designed to provide a robust response to the new strategic environment whilst remaining sufficiently responsive to further development.

Systematic planning for effective implementation of the defence strategy and the security policy is the essence of planning for defence. The strategic and technological environment assessment based on the harmonised perception of experts, from all the concerned ministries and departments forms the basis for evolving the strategy. Planning for defence is a multi disciplinary exercise involving, inter alia, an assessment and understanding of the trends in the international security environment, foreign policy, economic and international relations and the internal security environment.

Given India's size and security concerns, the outlay on defence, assessed either as a percentage of the total central government expenditure or of the gross domestic-product, continues to be one of the lowest amongst neighbouring countries.

The book contains the defence programmes of India and should be useful to administrators, policy makers, defence personnel and researchers alike.

Author

Contents

1

Introduction

India's defence policy aims at promoting and sustaining durable peace in the subcontinent, and equipping the defence forces adequately to safeguard aggression. The supreme command of the armed forces is vested in the President of India. The responsibility for national defence, however, rests with the cabinet. The Defence Minister is responsible to parliament for all matters concerning defence. Administrative and operational control of the armed forces is exercised by the Ministry of Defence and the three services headquarters.

Army

At the Army Headquarters in New Delhi, the Chief of the Army Staff is assisted by the Vice-Chief of the Army Staff and seven other Principal Staff Officers, namely, the two Deputy Chiefs of the Army Staff, Adjutant General, Quarter-Master General, Master General of Ordnance, Military Secretary, and Engineer-in-Chief.

The Army is organised into five operational Commands, *viz.,* Southern, Eastern, Western, Central and Northern Command and one Training Command. Each Command is under a General Officer Commanding-in-Chief who holds the rank of Lieutenant General. General Officer Commanding-in-Chief commanding an operative command is the commander of a demarcated geographical area and has both field and static formations under the command. The major field formations are Corps, Division and Brigade commanded by a General Officer Commanding of the rank of Lieutenant

General, a General Officer Commanding of the rank of Major General and Brigadier, respectively. The major static formations are Area, Independent Sub-Area and Sub-Areas. An area is commanded by a General Officer Commanding of the rank of Major General, and an independent sub-area and sub-area by a Brigadier.

The army consists of a number of arms and services. These are Armoured Corps, Regiment of Artillery, Corps of Air Defence Artillery, Army Aviation Corps, Corps of Engineers, Corps of Signals, Mechanised Infantry, Infantry, Army Service Corps, Military Nursing Service, Army Medical Corps, Army Dental Corps, Army Ordnance Corps, Corps of Electrical and Mechanical Engineers, Remount and Veterinary Corps, Military Farms Service, Army Education Corps, Intelligence Corps, Corps of Military Police, Judge Advocate General Department, Army Physical Training Corps, Pioneer Corps, Army Postal Service, Territorial Army, and Defence Security Corps. In addition, the army has its own Recruiting Organisation, Record Offices, Depots, Boys Establishments and Selection Centres and Training institutions.

NAVY

The navy is responsible for defence and security of India's maritime interests and assets, both in times of war and peace. The Chief of the Naval Staff at the Naval Headquarters, New Delhi, is assisted by four Principal Staff Officers, namely, the Vice-Chief of Naval Staff, Deputy Chief of Naval Staff, Chief of Personnel, and Chief of Material.

The navy has three commands, *i.e.,* Western, Eastern and Southern, with their headquarters located at Mumbai, Vishakhapatnam and Kochi respectively. Each command is headed by a Flag Officer Commanding-in-Chief in the rank of Vice-Admiral. Western Command and Eastern Command have under them operational fleets, *i.e.,* Western and Eastern Fleets comprising warships, submarines, aircraft and other support ships. Southern Naval Command is responsible for all training activities of the Indian Navy.

The Indian navy is a well-balanced three-dimensional force consisting of sophisticated missile-capable warships, aircraft carriers, minesweepers, advanced submarines and the latest aircraft in its inventory. Many of the warships are of indigenous design and have been constructed in Indian shipyards. These ships compare well with the ships of similar capability constructed by the advanced countries. The naval forces are maintained and supported by modern dockyard facilities encompassing state-of-the-art technology. At present, it has two major naval bases at Mumbai and Vishakhapatnam.

COAST GUARD

The Coast Guard came into being on 1 February 1977, and was constituted as an independent armed force of the Union of India with the enactment of CG Act 1978 on 18 August 1978. The Coast Guard's broad charter of duties includes: (a) Safety and protection of offshore installations and artificial islands: (b) Providing protection to fishermen in distress; (c) Protection of maritime environment; (d) Assisting Customs in anti-smuggling operations; (e) Enforcement of MZI Act; and (f) Safety of life and property at sea.

The general superintendence, direction and control of the Coast guard is exercised by the Director General Coast Guard under the Ministry of Defence.

The entire coastline of India and the national maritime zones have been divided into three Coast Guard Regions, namely, Western, Eastern and Andaman and Nicobar Islands, under the respective Commanders of the regions. The Regional Headquarters are located at Mumbai, Chennai and Port Blair.

The coast guard regions are divided into eleven Coast Guard Districts based in our maritime states. There are five District Headquarters on the west coast, namely, Porbandar, Mumbai, Goa, New Mangalore and Kochi. Four on the east coast, namely, Chennai, Vishakhapatnam, Paradip and Haldia, and two District headquarters in Andaman and Nicobar Islands, namely, Diglipur and Campbell Bay. In addition, there are coast guard stations and Air Enclaves at various locations.

Beginning with two frigates and five Seaward Defence Boats (SDBs), the coast guard service has made rapid progress in the last 20 years. The service has now developed into a full-fledged maritime organisation with nine Offshore Patrol Vessels (OPVs), two Advanced Offshore Patrol Vessels (AOPVs), 24 Fast Patrol Vessels (FPVs), 15 Interceptor Boats (IBs) and ICs, 17 Dornier Aircrafts and 15 Chetak Helicopters. The third Advanced Offshore Vessel is expected to be commissioned shortly.

AIR FORCE

The air force is organised both on functional and geographical basis. There are five operational commands. These are: Western Air Command, South-Western Air Command, Central Air Command, Eastern Air Command and Southern Air Command. In addition, Maintenance Command and Training Command are two functional commands.

At the Air Headquarters in New Delhi, the Chief of the Air Staff is assisted by the Vice-Chief of Air Staff, Deputy Chief of the Air Staff, Air Officer In-charge Personnel, Air Officer In-charge Administration, Air Officer In-charge Maintenance, and Inspector General (Flight Safety and Inspection). Each of these Principal Staff Officers is assisted by Assistant Chiefs of the Air Staff.

Today, the air force has an array of modern aircraft on its inventory besides other high-tech electronic and support equipment. The aircraft fleet consists of fighter bombers, air superiority fighters, interceptors, transport and logistic aircraft and helicopters. The fighter force comprises MiG-21 variants, MiG-23s, MiG-25s, MiG-27s and Jaguars which represent the modern generation strike aircrafts. Older generation aircrafts like the Hunters and Canberras are presently used in training and ancillary roles. MiG-29s and Mirage-2000 are air defence aircraft of the present generation. The transport fleet consists of IL-76s, AN-32s, the indigenously produced HS-748, Dornier-228 which are manufactured under licence by HAL and Boeing-737 are used for VIP duties. While the IL-76s provides the Air Force with heavy-lift capabilities, AN-32s and HS-748s are also used in training role besides performing air maintenance and communication duties. The helicopter fleet consists of Chetak, Cheetah, MI-8s, MI-17s and the heavy lift MI-26. All these aircraft are used for high-altitude operations and provide logistics support to our ground forces. Chetak/ Cheetah helicopters manufactured by HAL for the Air Force, are also used in Anti-Tank Guided Missile (ATGM) carriers, airborne Forward Air Controller (FAC) and for search and rescue operations. MI-8 Helicopters are specially modified to undertake tasks in Antarctica. In addition, the force has been supplemented with MI-25 and MI-35 attack helicopters. HPT-32 and HJT-16 (Kiran) aircraft, both manufactured by HAL, are used as basic and applied-stage trainers respectively, with the Kiran being supplemented by Polish Iskara aircraft. The first batch of women pilots were commissioned on 17 December 1994. Since then women pilots have been serving in frontline air force transport and helicopter squadrons. Women officers are also serving in technical, administrative, logistics, education and medical branches. The first batch of women Air Traffic Controller and Fighter Controller/DATS was commissioned in May 1996. Thus all branches of the IAF now have women serving.

COMMISSIONED RANKS

The following are the commissioned ranks in the three services; each rank is shown opposite its equivalent in the other service:

Army	*Navy*	*Air Force*
General	Admiral	Air Chief Marshal
Lieutenant General	Vice Admiral	Air Marshal
Major General	Rear Admiral	Air Vice Marshal
Brigadier	Commodore	Air Commodore
Colonel	Captain	Group Captain
Lieutenant Colonel	Commander	Wing Commander
Major	Lieutenant Commander	Squadron Leader
Captain	Lieutenant	Flight Lieutenant
Lieutenant	Sub-Lieutenant	Flying Officer

RECRUITMENT

The armed forces symbolise the unity of the country and the ideals of national integration. Recruitment to the armed forces is open to all Indian nationals, irrespective of caste, creed, community, religion and region. The endeavour has been to provide free and equal opportunities to all sections of the population to join the armed forces and render service in accordance with the ideals of secularism, democracy and social justice. India's armed forces offer challenging openings to our youth.

A remarkable feature of recruitment to the armed forces is that it is entirely voluntary. The competition for entry into the service is intense, reflective of the increasing numbers of educated youth in the country, coupled with the attractive terms and conditions of service, and the high level of respect commanded by the armed forces. Recruitment is made from different states/union territories on the basis of their recruitable male population. Conscious efforts are made to take care of the special needs of the border areas and hilly and other remote areas, by lowering educational and certain other criteria to suit their requirements.

INDUCTION OF WOMEN INTO THE ARMED FORCES

While provision has all along existed for women to join the Armed Forces Medical Services, the Armed Forces Dental Services and the Military Nursing Service, Section 12 of the Army Act provided that women would not normally be eligible for enrolment in the army. Similar provisions also existed in the cases of the air force and the navy. However, in acknowledgement of the changing times, the government has approved the induction of women into selected non-combatant branches in the three forces. The entry of women has, however, been restricted to the officer cadres, and they are on Short Service Commission basis. Further continuance of schemes would be decided on the basis of the experience gained. In pursuance of this decision, several women officers have since joined the service, in the EME, Signals, Engineers, Army Education Corps, Army Ordnance Corps, Army Service Corps and in the Judge Advocate General Department.

The response to this entry was encouraging and the courses were almost fully subscribed. Therefore, the existing planned intake of 50 officers per annum has been increased to 100 per annum. In addition, the government has also approved grant of antedate seniority to those women officers who possess a technical qualification. Till date, 219 women officers have been commissioned in various arms/services.

RECRUITMENT OF COMMISSIONED OFFICERS

Entry into the officer cadres in the armed forces is primarily through the Union Public Service Commission (UPSC). Graduates are eligible to join the armed forces through an examination known as the Combined Defence Services Examination (CDSE) conducted by the UPSC twice a year. Candidates who qualify in the examination join the Indian Military Academy (IMA), the Air Force Academy, and the Naval Academy for pre-commission training. Individuals selected for Short Service Commission are trained at the Officers Training Academy.

The candidates seeking a career in the armed forces after completion of 10+2 general education join the National Defence Academy (NDA). UPSC holds an entrance examination twice a year for entry in the NDA. Candidates who qualify in this examination join the respective Service Academies, *viz.*, the Indian Military Academy (IMA) for the army, the Air Force Academy for the air force, and the Naval Academy for the navy, for their pre-commission training.

There is also direct entry of officers through the Service Selection Boards (SSBs) for the army and navy, and through the Air Force Selection Board for the air force, without any written examination by the UPSC. Candidates in the age-group of 20 to 27 years with engineering degree and post-graduates in specified subjects in the age-group of 23 to 27 years are eligible for interview by the respective selection boards of branches of the armed forces.

In July 1992, the government approved a University Entry Scheme, initially for a period of three years, for induction of engineering students in their final year/pre-final year into the army. This scheme is already operating in the air force and the navy. Engineering students of various disciplines studying in the final/pre-final years in recognised universities/ institutions are eligible for induction into the technical branches/services of the army as short-service commissioned officers with the rank of 2nd Lieutenants (now Lieutenants) under this scheme. Their salary, however, is paid in one lumpsum on their joining the IMA for training, on the successful completion of which they will be granted permanent commission in the army. An intake of 100 officers per year has been planned under this scheme.

In order to mitigate the shortage of Technical Officers (Engineering) in the army, the government also approved a Short Service Commission (Tech) Entry scheme. This envisages recruitment of qualified technical graduates through the SSBs and their enrolment in the Officers Training Academy (OTA), Chennai, after medical tests for a ten-month course. At the end of the course, the successful candidates will receive Short Service Commission. Thereafter, they will be governed by the rules applicable to the other short-service commissioned officers.

Recruitment of medical officers in the armed forces is done through two sources. All MBBS graduates passing from the Armed Forces Medical College, Pune, are granted Permanent Commission. Apart from this, postgraduates/ MBBS degree-holders passing from civilian medical colleges are selected through competitive examinations on an all-India basis, conducted by the Directorate General of Armed Forces Medical College, Pune, partly for grant of regular commission and partly for grant of short service commission.

The government has already approved a scheme of induction of NCC 'C' certificate holders to SSC (NT) stream only, through SSB interview without passing UPSC (CDS) examination. This scheme will help in improving the intake in this entry.

A special commissioned officers, entry scheme has been introduced in the army. Under this entry serving JCOs/NCOs/ ORs in the age-group of 30-35 years, with an Army Senior School Certificate Pass (Class XI CBSE pattern) qualification, will be eligible for commission after screening/selection through SSB and a medical board. The officers so commissioned will earn promotion up to the rank of Colonel. The officers will be employed in the unit as platoon commanders/sub-unit commanders or equivalent/QM job/ERE appointments, *etc.*, up to the rank of Major. They will retire at the age of 55 years, after serving for about 20-25 years as officers. The scheme will not only improve the career prospects of existing JCOs/NCOs/ORs but also help in making up for the deficiency of officers in the army.

RECRUITMENT OF OTHER RANKS IN ARMY AND NAVY

There are 12 Zonal Recruiting Offices (ZROs) and 58 Branch Recruiting Offices (BROs) spread throughout the country. In addition, there is an Independent Recruiting Office (IRO) at Delhi. In order to inform the potential candidates of the commencement of recruitment well in advance, extensive recruitment publicity is undertaken throughout the country, including in remote areas.

Recruitment rules provide for relaxation in respect of educational and physical standards to the candidates from certain specified backward, remote and tribal regions to give them due representation in the army. Special physical standards for certain classes/regiments/tribes and categories have been laid down. Besides, relaxation in physical qualifications is being provided to certain categories of candidates like those between 16 and 18 years of age-group, national/state-level sportsmen and one son in the case of every serving soldier, ex-serviceman and war widow.

AIRMEN

Recruitment of airmen to the Indian Air Force is done through the Central Airmen Selection Board located at the Air Force Station, New Delhi. There are 13 selection centres under this board and they make the necessary arrangements for the conduct of selection tests and the final enrolment. A pilot project has been undertaken for the direct recruitment of trained manpower from, the civil stream in the trades, such as clerks, drivers, and Surveyor Automated Cartography. Besides, direct recruitment of technically qualified civilian personnel as JCO (catering) has been introduced.

TERRITORIAL ARMY

The territorial army is a voluntary part-time civilian force which plays a useful role in the defence of the country. It was raised in 1949 and since its inception, has rendered valuable service to the nation. The territorial army consists of departmental and non-departmental TA units. The departmental TA units are raised from amongst the employees of government departments and public-sector undertakings. There are at present 27 departmental and 25 non-departmental TA units. The five ecological battalions are also part of the departmental TA units.

As a result of internal disturbances and terrorist activities in Punjab, Jammu and Kashmir and other states, and the prevailing conditions along our northern, eastern and western borders, the TA has of late been called upon to play an active role in assisting the local army formations in these areas. As a result of these demands, all the 25 infantry battalions (TA) have been embodied since 1990-91, for varying periods.

The five ecological battalions of TA (called Eco Task Forces) have continued their excellent work of environmental upgradation of the degraded areas in Rajasthan, Madhya Pradesh, Uttar Pradesh, and Jammu and Kashmir. In consultation with the Ministry of Environment and Forests several steps aimed at reducing the cost of these Eco Task Forces, without actually lowering their output or efficiency, have been taken up. A proposal to reorganise 16 infantry battalions (TA), initiated by the TA Directorate, has been approved by the Ministry of Defence.

NATIONAL CADET CORPS

The National Cadet Corps (NCC) established on 15 July 1948 has emerged as the single largest structured youth movement in India. It has 11.6 lakh boys and girls in the senior and junior divisions in the army, navy and air force wings. This strength covers four percent of the eligible student population in the country. The Director General, NCC, located at New Delhi controls and oversees various activities of the NCC through 16 NCC Directorates spread across the country. There is a Central Advisory Committee for the NCC to provide overall policy guidelines. NCC is manned by the service personnel, wholetime NCC officers, teachers/professors and civilians. One lecturer/teacher in each educational institution is appointed Associate NCC officer.

The NCC whose motto is 'Unity and Discipline' has the following aims: (a) To develop qualities of character, courage, comradeship, leadership, secular outlook, a spirit of adventure and sportsmanship, and the ideal of selfless service among the youth to make them useful citizens; (b) To create a human resource of organised, trained and motivated youth to provide leadership in all walks of life including the Armed Forces and to be always available for the service of the nation.

During 1997-98, 17 centrally organised camps were held. Forty National Integration Camps were conducted across the country in which nearly 49,885 cadets participated. A total of 4,99,677 cadets attended the annual training camps during 1997. The NCC has an ongoing youth exchange programme with Canada, Singapore, U.K., Bangladesh and Sri Lanka. A team of three officers and 24 cadets (12 boys and 12 girls) went to Canada; eight NCC cadets (four boys and four girls) visited United Kingdom; one officer and four NCC cadets (two girls and two boys) to air wing attended the NCC air wing programme at Singapore; one officer and two cadets (one boy and one girl) visited Australia for the first time to attend the youth exchange programme, one officer and four NCC cadets (two boys and two girls) participated in the naval programme of Singapore, and a team of two NCC cadets (one boy and one girl) went to Sri Lanka.

TRAINING INSTITUTIONS

Sainik schools

The scheme to establish Sainik Schools was started in 1961 to broadbase the recruitment to the officers cadre of the defence forces. Sainik schools are a joint venture of the central and state governments. At present 18 Sainik schools, one each in all major states, are managed by the Sainik Schools Society. Boys from a state which does not have a Sainik school of its own are admitted to schools located in adjoining states. Sainik Schools are fully residential and admit students in Classes VI and IX strictly in order of merit obtained in the All India Sainik School Entrance Examination held in February each year. These schools are affiliated to the Central Board of Secondary Education and follow the 10+2 pattern, in the science stream.

The pass percentage of Sainik School students in the Class X and XII CBSE examinations during the academic session 1996-97 was 98.6 percent and 86.7 percent respectively. Students from 110 Sainik Schools joined the NDA in 1997. So far 4,901 students from the Sainik Schools have joined the NDA. The tuition fee has been raised to Rs. 14,000 per annum from the academic session 1997-98.

National defence academy

The National Defence Academy (NDA), Khadagvasala, is a joint services institution for training young cadets as future officers of the defence services. The motto of the Academy is *Sewa Paramo Dharma* (Service Before Self). As part of their training, cadets are provided academic inputs. The syllabus of the Academy has been approved by the Jawaharlal Nehru University for the grant of BA/BSc. degree at the time of passing from the Academy. As on date, the strength of cadets is 1,870. This includes 71 cadets from Bhutan.

Indian military academy

The Indian Military Academy (IMA), Dehradun, established in 1932, caters to the training of cadets for commission into the army. The training enables the gentlemen cadets to develop intellectual, moral and physical qualities through basic military training and broad academic education; and qualities of dynamism, initiative and understanding which form the very basis of leadership, in war as well as in peace. The motto of the Academy is *Veerta Aur Vivek* (Valour and Wisdom). The present strength of the IMA is 1,207 gentlemen cadets which includes 23 gentlemen cadets from friendly countries. The Army Cadet College is a wing of IMA which caters to training of service cadets selected for commission. The academic format is similar to the NDA on the lines of 10+2+3 and the syllabus is common. On completion of the course these cadets also qualify for a BA/BSc degree, recognised by the Jawaharlal Nehru University.

Officer's training academy

The Officers' Training Academy (OTA), Chennai, imparts pre-commission training for the following courses: (a) Short service commission course of 44-weeks for university graduates who qualify in the union public service commission; (b) a course of six months for lady cadets (Women Special Entry Scheme); and (c) permanent commission on Special List (PCSL) to selected service candidates, who qualify after a training of four weeks. Authorised training strength of the Academy is 500. So far 297 lady cadets have been granted short service commission.

Rashtriya Indian military college

Education on public-school lines is imparted at the Rashtriya Indian Military College, Dehradun, principally for the boys who subsequently desire to join the NDA with a view to obtaining a commission in the Armed Forces. The college admits students in Class VIII through a written examination-cum-*viva voce* test conducted under the aegis of the state governments throughout India twice every year in February and August. The college has the distinction of having had on its rolls three Chiefs of Army Staff and a Chief of Air Staff.

National defence college

The National Defence College (NDC) was founded in 1960 to prepare senior defence and civil service officers for a comprehensive understanding of major problems of national security and strategy. The aim of the NDC course is to equip future planning of national strategy in the context of world polity. Commandant NDC and Senior Directing Staff (Foreign Services) participated in the Asia Regional Forum (ARF) Meeting of the heads of national defence colleges/Institutions held in Manila in September 1997. The Prime Minister addressed the participants of the 37th NDC course on 'India's Role in a Changing World'.

Army cadet college

The Army Cadet College is a wing of IMA which caters to the

training of service cadets selected for commission. The academic format is similar to the NDA on the lines of 10+2+3, and the syllabus is common. On completion of the course these cadets also qualify for a BA/BSc degree recognised by the Jawaharlal Nehru University.

Army school of physical training

The Army School of Physical Training (ASPT), Pune, established in 1947, is the cradle of physical and recreational training in the army. It has training infrastructure to impart systematic and comprehensive instructions on physical training. Selected candidates from all ranks of the army, students from the police, paramilitary forces and friendly foreign countries attend various courses on physical training and allied subjects at ASPT.

Other training centres and schools

The College of Combat, Mhow, conducts the higher command, senior command and junior command courses for army officers. It also conducts a Combined Operational Review and Evaluation (CORE) programme for selected senior officers of the rank of Major General and equivalent of the three Services once every year. The College of Military Engineering, Kirkee (Pune), imparts training to the officers and other ranks in all aspects of military engineering. Long courses of over two years duration are also conducted to train officers up to degree standards. The Military College of Telecommunication Engineering, Mhow, imparts basic and advanced technical training in telecommunications and signal tactics. The Armoured Corps Centre and School, Ahmednagar, conducts training in tactical handling of armoured fighting vehicles, driving and maintenance. The School of Artillery, Deolali, provides training in field branch artillery. The Air Defence Guided Missiles School at Gopalpur-on-sea trains personnel of the Air Defence Artillery. The High Altitude Warfare School located at Gulmarg and Sonmarg trains personnel in the art of mountain warfare including rock, snow and ice-craft. The Counter Insurgency and General Warfare School, Vairengate, trains officers and men in the art of combating insurgency.

The Mechanised Infantry Regimental Centre conducts basic and technical training for recruits of mechanised infantry. In addition, it runs basic and instructor courses on anti-tank guided missiles for officers, JCOs and other ranks of mechanised infantry. It also carries out conversion training of units when they are converted to mechanised infantry or when change in equipment is involved. The College of Materials Management, Jabalpur, imparts specialised training in materials management including ammunition and explosives and also in contemporary materials management techniques. Some of the other Army training centres and schools are Army Service Corps School, Bareilly; EME School, Vadodara; Military College of Electronics and Mechanical Engineering, Secunderabad; College of Defence Management, Secunderabad; Remount and Veterinary Corps Centre and School, Meerut; Army Education Corps Training College and Centre, Pachmari; Army School of Physical Training, Pune; Army/Air Transport School, Agra; Military Intelligence Training School and Depot, Pune; Army School of Mechanical Transport, Bangalore; Corps of Military Police Centre and School, Bangalore; Institute of Military Law, Kamptee; Armed Forces Medical College, Pune; Institute of National Integration, Pune, and Army Medical Corps Centre and School, Lucknow.

PRODUCTION AND SUPPLIES

The Department of Defence Production and The Department of Defence Supplies were merged in December 1984 to constitute the present Department of Defence Production and Supplies. The primary role of the department is to equip the Armed Forces of the country with the latest equipment and weaponry systems and to contribute to modernisation of the Armed Forces. This task is being undertaken through 39 ordnance factories and 8 defence publicsector undertakings.

Ordnance factories

The Ordnance Factory Organisation is the largest departmental undertaking engaged primarily in the production of defence hardware for the armed forces and paramilitary/police. At present 39 ordnance factories with a manpower of 1.48 lakh spread all over India operate a wide range of discipline and technologies and supply critical lethal as well as non-lethal stores to defence forces. Some of the important products are field guns, anti-aircraft guns, mortars, various small arms and ammunition for weapons and guns, rockets, projectiles, pyro-technics, bombs, grenades, mines, demolition charges, depth charges, infantry combat vehicles, battle tanks, transport trucks and patrol vehicles, high-altitude and combat clothing, optical and fire control instruments, engineering equipment, supply dropping equipment including parachutes, rubberised items, various knitted and woollen items like blankets, web equipment and a wide range of general stores. The OFB's bulk production today is 54.56 mm Indian small armed system.

Besides meeting the requirement of the army, OFB produces a range of products for the air force and navy including air-dropped bombs for air force. Liquid fuel required for successful flight trials of *Prithvi* and *Agni* missiles, igniters and copper liners for the warheads are also supplied during development/production of Prithvi missile.

The production of Ajeya tank (T-72) and Sarath (BMP-II), infantry combat vehicles are carried out at Heavy Vehicle Factory, Avadi, and Ordnance Factory, Medak, respectively. A sophisticated opto-electronic production unit has been set up at Dehradun to produce the opto-electronic fire control and night vision devices required for Ajeya tank (T-72-MI) and Sarath vehicle (BMP-II).

Productionisation of Main Battle Tank (MBT) *Arjun*, which has now been accepted by the army, is also being taken up. To meet the army's requirement of high calibre ammunition, a new ordnance factory is being set up in Bolangir district of Orissa. The state-of-the-art plants are expected to be commissioned in the current year. As part of diversification efforts, Vehicles Factory, Jabalpur (VFJ), has taken up modification and upgradation of the *Jonga* to cater to the civilian market, besides introduction of new generation transport vehicles for armed forces under technology collaboration.

Defence undertakings

The Defence Public Sector Undertakings (DPSUs) were

structured with a flexible form of operation, decentralised management and adequate operational autonomy so as to utilise the defence technological base to a wide and diversified range of applications, in addition to the basic task of catering to the needs of the armed forces.

Eight publicsector undertakings (PSUs) currently function under the Department of Defence Production and Supplies. These are Hindustan Aeronautics Limited (HAL), Bharat Electronics Limited (BEL), Bharat Earth Movers Limited (BEML), Mazagon Dock Limited (MDL), Garden Reach Ship builders and Engineers Limited (GRSE), Goa Shipyard Limited (GSL), Bharat Dynamics Limited (BDL) and Mishra Dhatu Nigam Limited (MIDHANI). The value of production of the defence PSUs during 1997-98 has been of the order of Rs 6,327 crore as against Rs 5,599 crore in 1996-97. The average value of sales by these PSUs during the last 5 years is Rs 5,017.8 crore.

The Hindustan Aeronautics Limited (HAL) was set up in 1964 with its corporate office at Bangalore. The company has 13 divisions located in six states. The principal functions of the company are to design, manufacture, repair and overhaul various types of aircraft helicopters and related aero-engines, avionics, instruments and accessories. HAL is currently manufacturing Jaguar, Dornier-228 and MiG-27M aircraft, Cheetah and Chetak helicopters and various types of aero-engines. HAL is also engaged in the design and development of an Advanced Light Helicopter (ALH). All divisions of HAL have obtained the ISO 9001/9000 certificate by the International Accreditation and Quality Agencies.

The Bharat Electronics Limited (BEL) was established in 1954. It is the country's premier electronics organisation, having nine manufacturing units located at Bangalore, Chennai, Hyderabad, Machilipatnam, Pune, Taloja, Panchkula, Ghaziabad and Kotdwara. Its corporate office is at Bangalore. BEL is engaged in the design, development and manufacture of sophisticated state-of-the-art electronic equipments for the use of defence services and paramilitary organisations. Other users are All India Radio, Doordarshan, Department of Telecommunications, Police, Meteorological

Department, and so on. It has a very wide range of over 350 products, comprising communication equipment, radars for military and civil use, optical and opto-electronic equipments, sound and vision broadcasting equipment and electronic components. All the manufacturing divisions of BEL are equipped with the most advanced test and measurement and quality-control facilities for NIL grade /international civilian standards. ISO 9002 accreditation has been achieved by almost all the manufacturing units of BEL.

Bharat Earth Movers Limited (BEML) was incorporated as a DPSU in May 1964 and commenced its operations in January 1965. It has three modern production units at Bangalore, Kolar Gold Fields and Mysore. Besides, a subsidiary unit, Vigyan Industries Limited (VIL) in Tarikere (Karnataka) has been established by taking over an existing venture of the state government. Its corporate office is at Bangalore. The company is presently engaged in the design, development and manufacture of a wide range of sophisticated equipments and systems, particularly earth-moving machines, rail coaches, track-laying equipments, heavy-duty trucks, trailers, diesel engines, and so on. BEML is a leader in the earth-moving industry with over 70 percent market share. Its equipments and systems are productively deployed in India and over 30 other countries across the globe. The company has acquired ISO 9000 certificate.

The Mazagon Dock Limited (MDL) is the country's leading shipbuilding yard and can build warships up to 6,000 DWT displacement and merchant ships up to 27,000 DWT. It has units at Mumbai, Nhava and Mangalore and headquarters at Mumbai. Its major activities include construction of submarines, missile-boats and destroyers, and so on for the Indian Navy and offshore-supply vessels and well-head platforms, and so on for the Oil and Natural Gas Commission (ONGC). The company also provides diving services as well as services for coating/laying sub-sea pipes. The Garden Reach Shipbuilders and Engineers Limited (GRSE) was established in 1884 as a small ship-repair workshop. It was taken over by the Government of India in the early 1960. It is a multi-unit shipyard-cum-general engineering company. It has six units in and around Calcutta and a Diesel Engine Plant at Ranchi (Bihar). Its corporate office is at Calcutta. It has three distinct divisions, namely, ship, engineering and engine divisions. It is presently engaged in the construction of warships and auxiliary vessels of various types for the navy and coast guard to undertake repair of vessels of these two organisations.

The activities of Goa Shipyards Limited (GSL) located at Vasco da Gama, primarily comprise construction and repair/ refit of ships/vessels. It has undertaken construction/refit of variety of vessels for the Indian navy and the coast guard as well as for the non-defence sector. It is currently building advanced offshore patrol vessels of in-house design.

The Bharat Dynamics Limited (BDL), Hyderabad, was established in 1970 to manufacture guided missiles. It has two units at Kanchanbagh and Bhanoor. It is also the prime production agency for missile weaponry systems. The company utilising the spare capacity available has diversified into small arms production to meet the requirement of paramilitary forces of the country.

The Mishra Datu Nigam Limited (MIDHANI) located at Hyderabad was incorporated in 1973. MIDHANI's product range includes super alloys, maraging steels, heat-resistance alloys, controlled expansion alloys, tungsten, molybdenum, and so on in a variety of all mill forms to serve the strategic needs of the country including, defence, atomic energy, spare aeronautics with a view to attaining self-reliance in this sophisticated field. The company has obtained ISO 9002 certificate for the entire plant.

RESEARCH AND DEVELOPMENT

The Defence Research and Development Organisation (DRDO) was established in 1958 by amalgamating the Defence Science Organisation and some of the Technical Development Establishments. A separate Department of Defence Research and Development was formed in 1980 which operates through a network of 50 laboratories/ establishments. The department is engaged in the pursuit of self-reliance in critical technologies of relevance to national security. It formulates and executes programmes of scientific research, design and development leading to induction of state-of-the-art weapons, platforms and other equipments required by the armed forces. It functions under the control of Scientific Adviser to the Defence Minister who is also Secretary, Defence Research and Development.

The major achievements towards indigenous development of defence weapons and systems are: (a) development leading to production of surface-to-surface missile, Prithvi; (b) state-of-the-art main battle tank, Arjun; (c) flight simulators for aircraft; (d) pilotless target aircraft, Lakshya; (e) parallel super-computer pace plus; and (f) small arms and ammunition.

The DRDO has acquired world class core competence in the area of guided missiles, super computer, UAV, armaments and ammunition including illuminating ammunition, night vision devices, secured communication, military bridging systems and fire detection and suppression systems. India is now self-reliant in armours, armaments, super computers and missile systems.

The DRDO has launched a 10-year national mission for enhancing self-reliance in defence systems with the goal of increasing the indigenous content in the annual defence acquisition from the level of 30 percent in the year 1995 to 70 percent by the year 2005.

It has also accorded high priority for development of systems in critical areas of technologies which have been denied by advance countries or which are likely to be denied in the future. The weapons and ammunition developed by the organisation and produced by production agencies include Indian field gun, INSAS rifle, LMG 5.56 mm, charge line mine-clearing for safe passage of vehicles in the battlefield, illuminating ammunition for enhancing night field-fighting capability, cluster weapon system for fighter aircraft, new generation bombs for high-speed aircraft, naval mines and 105 mm FSAPDS, 105 mm and 125 mm FSAPDS ammunition. Multibarrel rocket system *Pinaka* is undergoing user trial. In the area of electronics and instrumentation, the significant developments are low-level tracking radar *Indra*

I, Indra II for army and air force, lightweight field artillery radar, battlefield surveillance radar, secondary surveillance radar, avalanche victim detector, tidex, EW systems, night vision devices and secured telephone SECTEL, installation and commissioning of facilities and equipment for fabrication of Galleum Arsenide Wafers at GAETEC and artillery combat command and control systems.

Some of the development successes in the area of engineering systems are bridge layer tank *Kartik*, military bridging systems, various types of shelters, crash fire-tenders, rapid intervention vehicle and state-of-the-art fire-detection and suppression system for tanks, naval ships, missile launchers and barbette areas.

In the area of naval systems and materials the organisation has developed an advanced ship sonar system, the marine accoustic research ship *Sagardhwani,* underwater anti-fouling paints, torpedoes, naval simulators and jackal steels. The submarine sonar and weapon control system *Panchendriya is* getting ready for harbour/sea trials. The indigenous light combat aircraft (LCA) is getting ready for maiden flight trials by 1998. The advanced technology aero engine *Kaveri* of LCA is undergoing multi test-bed trials.

The Kaveri engine has been successfully tested for about 500 hours on multiple test beds. The remotely-piloted vehicle *Falcon* has successfully undergone 25 developmental flight trials and is getting ready for user trials. The Integrated Guided Missile Development Programme (IGMDP) comprises four missile systems, Prithvi, surface-to-surface tactical battle field missile; *Akash,* medium-range surface-to-air missile; *Trishul,* short-range surface-to-air missile; and *Nag*, third-generation anti-tank-missile. *Trishul is* getting ready for user trials. Akash and Nag are in advanced stages of development. The programme also included successful development of re-entry technology demonstrator under project *Agni*.

The department has developed preserved and convenience foods for the armed forces. State-of-the-art technologies developed for missile programme LCA and other high technology systems are being channelised to make available to the common man biomedical equipment at a fraction of the prevailing price of imported systems.

A society of biomedical technology has been formed for this purpose. Extra lightweight floor reaction orthosis (FROs) for polio-handicapped persons, cardiac stress analyser, cardiac pacemaker and cytoscan for early detection of cancer cells have been developed and the technology has been transferred to industry. In addition to the above, the Department has been rendering many services to the armed forces.

RESETTLEMENT AND WELFARE OF EX-SERVICEMEN

In order to maintain the youthful profile of the armed forces, over 55,000 service personnel are retired /released every year at a comparatively young age. As per statistics a total of 13.55 lakh ex-servicemen and 2.43 lakh widows have been registered with them and were reported to be surviving as on 31 December 1996.

The Directorate General of Resettlement (DGR) under the Ministry of Defence (MOD) has been set up to look after all matters connected with resettlement and welfare of ex-servicemen and their dependents. A Kendriya Sainik Board under the chairmanship of the Defence Minister has been established for laying down the general policy for the welfare of ex-servicemen and their dependents for the administration of welfare funds, and also for coordinating the work of the Sainik Boards in the country. At the state level, the Rajya Sainik Boards, and at the district level the Zila Sainik Boards, have been established. The Government of India bears 50 percent of the expenditure incurred on the organisations of Rajya and Zila Sainik Boards, the remaining expenditure being borne by the respective state governments.

Resettlement

Resettlement activities for the retired /retiring service personnel consist of the following: (a) Training programmes to reorient retiring defence personnel towards civil employment; (b) Providing re-employment opportunities in government/semi-government/public sector organisations; and (c) Schemes for self-employment.

Training

For retiring service officers the following training programmes were introduced during the year 1996-97: (a) Diploma in Industrial Security and Labour Laws; (b) Coaching for Airline Transport Pilot Licence/Senior Commercial Pilot Licence/Commercial Helicopter Pilot Licence; (c) Consultant in ISO-9000; (d) Quality Assurance Manager ISO-9000; (e) Deputy Quality Assurance Manager ISO-9000; (f) Consultancy as a career; (g) Equity and Portfolio Management; (h) LAN Engineering; and (j) POXPRO Oracle. During the training year 1996-97, 1,145 officers were trained. The vocational training, ITI training and on-the-job training are presently being conducted for retiring service personnel other than officers.

Re-employment

Re-employment constitutes a major means of rehabilitation or resettlement of ex-servicemen. To achieve this goal both the central and state governments have provided various concessions/ facilities. These include reservation of posts, relaxations in age/educational standards, priority in employment, and so on. The central government has reserved 10 percent of Group 'C' and 20 percent of Group 'D' posts for ex-servicemen in central ministries and departments. The percentage of reservation in publicsector undertakings and nationalised banks in these categories are 14.5 and 24.5 percent respectively. Besides, there is 10 percent reservation for the post of Assistant Commandant in paramilitary forces. Reservations under the state governments vary from two percent to 20 percent. There is no reservation for ex-servicemen in Bihar, Kerala and Meghalaya.

DGR has been nominating ex-servicemen security agencies to various PSUs and privatesector organisations. These security agencies provide employment opportunities for officers and other ranks. There are over 300 ex-servicemen security agencies which are registered with DRG, of which 130 have been sponsored for work. This alone has generated employment opportunities for over 7,000 ex-servicemen and over 400 officers.

The concept of Ecological Task Force was mooted in 1992 for the purpose of restoring the forest cover in regions where significant deforestation had taken place. These units were initially raised in three states, namely, Uttar Pradesh, Rajasthan and Jammu and Kashmir.

The task forces are manned by ex-servicemen who are paid salaries as per territorial army scales. Every individual, irrespective of his rank prior to retirement, is re-employed as a sepoy. The Ministry of Defence provides officers to command these units.

SCHEMES FOR SELF-EMPLOYMENT

Important schemes for self-employment for ex-servicemen are SEMFEX-I, SEMFEX-II and SEMFEX-III. These schemes have been launched in collaboration with the Small Industries Development Bank of India, NABARD, and the Khadi and Village Industries Commission for providing extensive self-employment opportunities for ex-servicemen and their dependents.

Under SEMFEX-I scheme launched in April 1987 financial assistance is provided to ex-servicemen to set up small industrial projects for self-employment. Loans under this Scheme are provided by the respective State Financial Corporation. As on 31 December 1996 there were 6,697 beneficiaries and the amount sanctioned was to the tune of Rs 179.48 crore since inception.

The SEMFEX-II scheme was launched in January 1988 by the DGR in collaboration with the National Bank for Agricultural and Rural Development (NABARD) to provide assistance for agricultural and allied activities. Under the scheme, financial assistance up to Rs 10 lakh for setting up of industrial units/service establishments is given. The ceiling of Rs 10 lakh is, however, not applicable for setting up of units relating to agro-industries and non-agro industries and they can be supported up to SSI limit under non-farm sector activities. However, all agro and food processing units including processing of forest produce will be assisted without any ceiling on the project cost.

Eligible borrowers may also be financed for acquisition of a maximum of two transport vehicles. Interest-free soft loan assistance for all schemes under non-farm sector as also the innovative hi-tech projects, export-oriented units and agro-processing projects are covered under the farm sector. Since inception and up to December 1996 loans amounting to Rs 2,057.82 crone have been sanctioned to 3,550 beneficiaries.

The SEMFEX-III scheme was launched in October 1991 in collaboration with the Khadi and Village Industries Commission (KVIC) but was implemented from 1992-93. It provides self-employment opportunities for setting up village industries in the purview of KVIC. Under this scheme, ex-servicemen and their widows are eligible to take up self-employment ventures.

Financial assistance for such ventures is provided under a liberalised pattern of assistance by the KVIC. Margin money requirement is only five percent of the project cost. The project proposals up to Rs. 25 lakh will be financed under the scheme. Grant up to 30 percent will be provided for the project cost up to Rs 10 lakh and 10 percent for the remaining cost of the project. The KVIC has earmarked 10 percent of the states allocated budget under the Scheme. The loan granted to village industries under this scheme carries an annual rate of interest of 17 percent and 4 percent on loan for khadi units. The scheme is picking up. Up to December 1996, a loan of Rs 295.33 lakh was sanctioned to 467 beneficiaries.

Welfare

Kendriya Sainik Board (KSB) is responsible for progress in the various welfare benefits and concessions provided, by Central and state governments to ex-servicemen, war widows, disabled ex-servicemen and dependents. The undermentioned concessions and facilities are available to eligible personnel: (i) Re-possession of land/house owned by ex-servicemen which they had rented out during their service career; (ii) Children of defence personnel killed or disabled in action or disabled, who are studying in educational institutions under the Department of Education of both central and state governments, are entitled to total exemption from tuition fee and other fees levied by the institutions.

Grants are provided to meet hostel charges towards cost of books, stationery and uniform where it is compulsory; (iii) 25 seats in the MBBS, one seat in BDS and two seats in engineering are available through KSB for wives/widows and wards of those servicemen killed in action, disabled in action and boarded out from service, died while in service with death attributable to military service, died while in service and boarded out with disability, attributable to service and Gallantry Award winners; (iv) 25 percent seats are reserved for the wards of serving and ex-service personnel in Sainik Schools; (v) States/UTs have made reservation of seats in professional colleges/ITI/polytechnics for wards of serving and retired defence personnel; (vi) A grant of Rs 600 p.m. per student is provided to wards of war-bereaved, disabled and attributable peacetime casualties housed in 35 war memorial hostels, to enable them to pursue their studies; (vii) Ex-servicemen, their families and families of deceased service personnel drawing pension of any kind are entitled to free out-patient treatment in military hospitals subject to certain conditions. In addition to the existing military hospitals, 24 MI rooms and 12 dental centres have been specially created from the funds provided by the services and KSB for providing medical facilities to ex-servicemen pensioners and their dependents.

Ex-servicemen suffering form serious diseases are provided 60 percent reimbursement of the total expenditure for treatment in civil hospitals in case they have not been provided assistance from other sources. Assistance for dialysis is restricted to Rs 75,000 only; (viii) 75 percent concession in rail fare for travel in 11 Class is available to war-widows including those of IPKF casualties, on production of I card issued by KSB. In addition, the government of India has announced free travel for recipients of Gallantry Award (*Chakra* Series only) in first class/II AC throughout the country. The passes are issued by the office of the divisional railway manager. fifty percent concession in fare for air travel in domestic rights of the Indian Airlines, is available to the recipients of *Param Vir Chakra, Maha Vir Chakra, Ashok Chakra and Kirti Chakra* and permanently disabled officers who have been invalidated out of service, and dependent members of their families; (ix) Financial assistance form *Raksha Mantri's* Discretionary Fund (RMDF) is provided to ex-servicemen and widows of ex-servicemen in penury, for marriage of daughters, education of children, repair of house and medical assistance; (x) The majority of states have made reservations for serving/retired armed forces personnel in allotment of house sites/houses; (xi) Financial assistance is provided to war-widows/ war-disabled for repair of houses on 50 percent cost sharing basis with state governments up to a maximum of Rs 10,000; (xii) Over 252 Sainik rest-houses have been created in the country which provide transit facilities to ex-servicemen and dependents at nominal rates; and (xiii) The states/UTs provide cash award/annuity/cash in lieu of land for gallantry/ non-gallantry award winners.

Armed forces flag day fund

Before April 1993 there were four separate funds, namely, Amalgamated Special Fund for War-Bereaved, War-Disabled and other ex-Servicemen /serving personnel; (ii) Flag Day Fund; (iii) St. Dunstan's (India) and KSB Fund; and (iv) Indian Gorkha Ex-servicemen's Welfare Fund. These separate funds have been merged into an Armed Forces Flag Day Fund. A number of welfare schemes are funded from the Armed Forces Flag Day Fund administered by the Kendriya Sainik Board.

The fund has a corpus of Rs 54.73 crore as on 31 March 1997, and the interest earned on the investment of the corpus is utilised for various welfare activities/schemes approved by the managing committee of the fund. Financial assistance is also provided to institutions such as military hospitals, paraplegic homes at Kirkee and Mohali, Red Cross Society, Cheshire Homes, St. Dunstans After Care Organisation (for the blind).

Concessions to ex-servicemen

The concessions provided to the ex-servicemen *inter alia* include: (a) Free education for children of armed forces personnel killed or disabled in action; (b) Reservation of 25 seats in MBBS and one seat in BDS to the wards of ex-servicemen killed in action, disabled and boarded out, died in service, where death is attributable to military service and so on; (d) eservation of seats in professional colleges by various states/Uts for wards of serving and retired armed forces personnel; (e) Grant of Rs 400 pm to wards of war-bereaved, housed in 35 war memorial hostels; and (f) Financial assistance from RM's discretionary funds to old and infirm ex-servicemen and their widows in indigent circumstances.

In addition, the ex-servicemen have also been extended the following facilities: (i) The Ministry of Railways has issued instructions to the GMs of all Indian railways for allowing the benefit of two complimentary passes in 2nd AC/1st class to the service personnel/ex-servicemen who have won gallantry awards like *Param Vir Chakra, Maha Vir Chakra* and *Vir Chakra; (ii)* Ex-servicemen are entitled for free medical treatment from the military hospitals. If not treated from the military hospitals they are granted financial assistance equal to 60 percent of total expenditure for treatment of serious diseases.

Funds have also been provided for procurement of the intraocular lenses for ex-servicemen; (iii) The ex-servicemen and their families are entitled to the CSD (1) canteen facilities available in units/establishments; (iv) *Saini Bhawans*/rest-houses have been provided in selected centres for the stay of the ex-servicemen who visit these places in connection with settlement of their problems; and (v) The Indira Awaas Yojana has been extended to the families of servicemen and paramilitary forces killed in action irrespective of the income criteria subject to the condition that; (a) they reside in rural areas, (b) they have not been covered under any other shelter rehabilitation scheme; and (c) they are houseless or in need of shelter or shelter upgradation.

2

National Security Environment

There is a greater international acceptance of the compelling logic for India to develop a credible minimum deterrent against the use or the threat of use of weapons of mass destruction. India's approach is aimed at greater regional and international stability and is entirely in consonance with its consistent efforts towards the ultimate elimination of all weapons of mass destruction. This global disarmament process has to be based on universal and non-discriminatory treaties and on the principles of equal security for all.

Emergence of ideology-linked terrorism, abetment of and support to separatist insurgencies in other countries, economic crises and the spread of small arms are some of the factors that link India's security directly with its extended neighbourhood. This security overlap particularly includes India's neighbouring countries and the regions of Central Asia, South-East Asia, the Gulf and the Indian Ocean. India has a direct stake in the security of this entire region but is not hemmed in by it.

India's national security objectives are served by:

a) Defending the country's borders as defined by law and enshrined in the Constitution and protecting the lives and property of its citizens against terrorism and insurgencies.

b) Having a secure, effective and credible minimum deterrent against the use or threat of use of weapons of mass destruction against India. The profile of this deterrent, including accurate and refined delivery systems, will not be circumscribed in range and payload by any outside pressure or influence but will be determined by the country's threat perception at any point of time.

c) Insulating the country from the effect of individual or group restrictions on the transfer of material, equipment and technologies that have a bearing on India's security, particularly its defence preparedness. This involves a greater emphasis on in-house research, development and production of the nation's requirements and recourse to feasible alternative sources.

d) Promoting further cooperation and understanding with neighbouring countries and implementing mutually-agreed confidence-building measures.

e) Working with countries of the Non-Aligned Movement to address key challenges before the international community and engaging in co-operative security initiatives such as the ASEAN Regional Forum (ARF).

f) Pursuing security and strategic dialogues with major powers and key partners.

g) Following a consistent and principled policy on disarmament and international security issues based on the principles of supreme national interest, universality, non-discrimination and equal security for all.

INDIA'S NEIGHBOURS

China is India's largest neighbour. India's relations with Chine have improved in recent years. India has expressed its interest time and again in resolving the boundary dispute with China peacefully and through bilateral negotiations as quickly as possible. China's assistance to Pakistan's nuclear weapons programme and the transfer of missiles and missile technology to Pakistan affect the security situation in South Asia. India does not regard China as an adversary but as a great neighbour with which it would like to develop mutually beneficial and friendly relations.

Exchanges at the governmental, parliamentary, non-governmental, people-to-people and other levels have continued during the year. The first ever visit by a Chief of General Staff of the Chinese People Liberation Army to India took place from April 26 May 1, 1998. India's Deputy Chairman, Planning Commission, met the Chinese Foreign Minister during the ASEAN Regional Forum (ARF)-Post Ministerial Conference (PMC) Meeting in Manila on July 27, 1998. Such high-level political and military contacts serve the objective of furthering mutual understanding between the two countries and reassuring each other about their peaceful intentions.

The Agreement on the Maintenance of Peace and Tranquillity Along the Line of Actual Control in the India-China Border Areas signed on September 7, 1993 and the Agreement between the Government of the Republic of India and the Government of the People's Republic of China on Confidence-Building Measures in the Military Field Along the Line of Actual Control in the India-China Border Areas signed on November 29,1996 provide a reliable framework for the maintenance of peace and tranquillity in the border areas.

Prime Minister, Atal Behari Vajpayee's landmark visit to Lahore on February 20-21, 1999 on the inaugural run of the Delhi-Lahore bus service, once again demonstrated India's deep desire for peaceful, friendly and cooperative relations with Pakistan. It is significant that in the Lahore Declaration the two countries condemned terrorism in all its forms and manifestations and affirmed their resolve to combat the menace. The two countries also undertook, in the Lahore Declaration, to refrain from intervention and interference in each other's internal affairs.

A Memorandum of Understanding was signed by the Foreign Secretaries in the presence of the Prime Ministers in Lahore on February 21, 1999. The MU identifies measures aimed at promoting an environment of peace and stability between the two countries. These measures include bilateral consulations, advance notification of ballistic missile flight tests, reducing the risks of accidental or unauthorised use of nuclear weapons and improvement of communication links between the defence establishments of the two sides. These steps would contribute in a tangible way to the objective of fostering a climate of stability and security in the region.

During the Defence Secretary-led talks on the Siachen Glacier issue in New Delhi in November 1998, the Indian side made concrete suggestions that aimed at establishing a regime of peace and tranquity in a limited area of the state of Jammu & Kashmir, which is an intergral part of India in its entirety, through a ceasefire, freezing the present ground positions and working out a bilateral mechanism to monitor the ceasfire. Along with political initiatives taken by the government, the altreness of India's security forces has managed to contain the level of militancy. The effective and coordinated action by the security forces has led to the elimination of over 3,000 militants since 1996 and the arrest of over 6,500 in the same period in the Jammu & Kashmir sector.

India's relations with its other neighbours have a strong security dimension since mutual understanding and coordinated action of these countries with India can lead to the eventual establishment of peace and stability in the region for the benefit of all the South Asian countries. India has traditionally enjoyed close and stable ties of friendship and cooperation with both Nepal and Bhutan. High-level interactions have provided direction and impetus to the wide-ranging and multifaceted cooperation between India and these countries.

The state visit of the President of India to Nepal in April 1998 and that of His Majesty, the King of Nepal, to India as the Chief Guest at Republic Day Celebrations in January 1999 were an important landmarks in our relations with that country. Cooperation on security related issues is monitored through regular meetings of the joint working group on border management and Home Secretary level talks which has helped coordinate the efforts of both countries in managing the long open border between them and to prevent its misuse by elements acting against the interests of either country.

Priority has also been attached to the consolidation of the close cooperation between the armed forces of the two countries. The official visit of His Majesty the King of Bhutan to India in October 1998 was another milestone in the tradition of frequent high-level contacts between India and Bhutan, and provided an opportunity for a comprehensive and wide-ranging review of the bilateral relationship. Regular dialogues with Bhutan have also resulted in close coordination and cooperation on security related issues of interest to both countries.

With Bangladesh the dialogue on security and border management was sustained during the year. Talks between the two countries at the level of Home Secretary and the border security forces complemented the exchanges between the Chiefs of Staff of India and Bangladesh. Issues covered during these talks related to security, insurgency, illegal immigration and border management. India has maintained a regular dialogue with Myanmar on areas of mutual interest in security such as border management and drugs trafficking.

India continued to pursue a policy of the development of close bilateral relations based on friendship, mutual understanding and trust with Sri Lanka and Maldives. India remains supportive of a peaceful, political solution to the internal conflicts in Sri Lanka consistent with a long-term commitment to the sovereignty, unity and integrity of the country. The warmth and cooperative spirit of India's relations with Maldives translate into common endeavours in defence-related areas such as training, supply of equipment and the maintenance of a high level dialogue between the political leadership and defence officials of the two countries.

EAST AND SOUTH EAST ASIA

India's relations with South East Asia have made considerable progress. As a full dialogue partner of the ASEAN and as a member of the ASEAN Regional Forum (ARF), India has been engaged more closely than in the past with efforts to promote regional and international security. The essential mutuality of interests between India and ASEAN countries has been reflected in the deliberations of the several conferences and workshops under the ARF process. This was evident at the 5th ARF meeting held in July 1998 after the Indian nuclear tests in May 1998. India expects to continue to make a constructive contribution to this process and to benefit from this interaction in keeping with close bilateral relations with each of the ASEAN countries. India is also keen on developing mutually beneficial defence-related linkages with countries of the ASEAN and the Pacific regions, such as visit of naval ships, training of service personnel, repair facilities for military equipment, spare parts supplies and joint development of equipment and technologies required by the armed forces. India and Malaysia have a mechanism for a structured bilateral defence dialogue on an annual basis. The launching of Bangladesh-India-Myanmar-Sri Lanka-Thailand-Economic Cooperation (BIMSTEC) grouping in June 1997 has created additional linkages and scope for cooperation between some member countries of the ASEAN with some from the SAARC.

CENTRAL ASIA

Violent conditions in Afghanistan continued the sufferings of the Afghan people; they also complicated the regional security environment. The Taliban success in Northern Afghanistan including their occupation of Mazar-e-Sharif (August 10) and Bamyian (mid-September) increased the area under Taliban advance but was also able to recapture some territories gained by the Taliban, especially in the Takhar province.

The events of 1998 also made it abundantly clear that the military resolution to the Afghan situation was not possible. The situation in Afghanistan further contributed adversely to the regional security situation through the existence of terrorist camps and the export of narcotics. India which has major security interest in Afghanistan continued to monitor the Afghan situation very closely. As a neighbouring country with a land border with Afghanistan, India remains committed to its unity, sovereignty, territorial integrity and independence. It believes that a solution to the Afghan situation can only be found through negotiations which would lead to the establishment of a broadbased government with the participation of all ethnic groups. The Central Asian countries and India have a common stake in countering negative phenomena such as religious extremism, terrorism, ethnic conflicts, and so on. Bilateral contacts with the countries of Central Asia at the political level, and sustaining a dialogue through governmental and non-governmental channels on security issues is a regular feature of bilateral relations.

In 1997 India, Iran and Turkmenistan signed a trilateral transit agreement to facilitate trade with Central Asia. India has also participated with a positive and constructive approach in regional security initiatives such as the Conference on Interaction and Confidence-Building in Asia (CICA).

WEST ASIA, NORTH AFRICA AND THE GULF

Developments in the Pesian Gulf region directly impinge on India's security interests. It is a primary source of India's energy needs, including crude oil, petroleum, petroleum-products and gas, and will remain so in the foreseeable future. India also has very substantial other economic interests in the region, with annual bilateral trade exceeding US$ 10 billion and yearly foreign exchange remittances in excess of US $ 4 billion. A strong Indian community resides in the region reinforcing its civilisation links with India and contributing to the economic life of the countries where they live. Bilateral visits at the Chiefs of Staff have been exchanged with the Persian Gulf and West Asian countries.

During this year Indian navy ships have visited Oman, Saudi Arabia, UAE, Iran and Bahrain. The aircraft carrier *Virat*, accompanied by other ships visited the Gulf region in March 1999. These goodwill visits underscore India's abiding interest in and friendship for the countries of the region. India is vitally interested in peace and development in the West Asian region. India believes that a just, comprehensive and lasting peace in the region can only be established on the basis of UN Security Council Resolutions and the principle of 'Land for Peace.' India welcomed the Wye River Memorandum of Understanding signed between Israel and the PLO on October 23, 1998 in Washington DC to facilitate implementation of the Interim Agreements.

With some countries in West Asia & North Africa, India and has concluded bilateral agreements to combat terrorism and organised crime and to give a global focus to this problem. The West Asia and North Africa region is economically important also as bulk of phosphate and phospheric acid is imported from here.

INDIAN OCEAN REGION

India's maritime interests in the Indian Ocean region stem from a geopolitical and economic reality. A coastline of 7,683 kms, and EEZ of 2.01 million sq. kms, the movement by sea of a substantial part of India's external trade and the need to protect the island territories of India, are some of the factors which determine the strategic importance of the Indian Ocean region to India's security. India's active participation in the Indian Ocean Rim Association for Regional Cooperation is part of an effort to develop mutually beneficial relations with key countries of the region.

India continues to attach high importance to cooperation with the navies of South-East Asian and other Indian Ocean states. India also has cooperative programmes such as bilateral exercises with important maritime powers of the world. India would be taking part in *Blue Crane* exercises in co-operation with South Africa and other SADC countries. This participation would be of a tri-Service nature. The Indo-South African Joint Committee on Defence held its first meeting in August 1998 in Pretoria. There has also been a frequent exchange of visits at the level of Chiefs of Staff of the services.

P-5 COUNTRIES

India and Russia have taken determined steps to raise bilateral defence cooperation to a level of strategic partnership between the two countries. There is a considerable overlap in the security perspectives of the two countries on key regional and international issues. On a bilateral plane defence cooperation between the two encompasses a strategic dialogue, defence supplies and interaction between defence production and R&D facilities. This cooperation is anchored on a deep understanding and appreciation of each other's security concerns and priorities.

In December 1998, India and Russia signed a bilateral agreement on cooperation in the military-technical sphere until the year 2010. The programmes of cooperation under this agreement are designed to meet the futuristic requirements of both parties. Other dimensions of ongoing cooperation with Russia include service-to-service exchanges, ship visits and military training.

The development of India's relations with France is reflective of the increasing ties with individual countries of Western Europe and the European Union. The Defence Minister, George Fernandes, visited France from January 11 to 14, 1999. The discussions reinforced the determination of the two countries to strengthen and diversify defence cooperation between India and France and underscored the common philosophical underpinning of the approach of India and France to contemporary challenges confronting the international community.

The Indo-French High Committee on Defence met in May 1998, commencing a broad strategic dialogue between the two sides. India expects to develop relations with other countries of Western Europe also on the principles of mutual benefit, mutual respect and a mutual understanding of each other's security concerns and priorities.

Regular substantive high-level political dialogue and close economic interaction between India and the countries of Western Europe individually and the European Union (EU) as a whole continued during this period. There have been moves towards opening a discussion on NATO's nuclear doctrine and its scope of activities, even as it prepares to accept three new members from next year. The continuing exchange of high level visits between India and the countries of Western Europe, the political dialogue with the EU Troika and the strengthening of economic linkages, represents the interest on both sides in intensifying bilateral cooperation for mutual benefit. India has a continuing interest in improving bilateral defence cooperation with USA based on mutual respect, mutual benefit, equality and understanding.

Although there have been sporadic contacts between high level military officials since May 1998, the institutional framework for cooperation that had evolved over the years including the Defence Policy Group, the Joint Technical Group and Steering Groups at the service-to-service level remains suspended by the USA. India hopes for an early revival of normal defence ties. India and USA are engaged in a high-level dialogue to bring about greater convergence on security issues. During these talks, India has reiterated its balanced and constructive approach on security matters within the framework of its vital security interests. However, like the United States, India will be guided by its supreme national interests in defining its essential security requirements without unacceptable constraints and limitations.

INDIA'S NUCLEAR POLICY, DISARMAMENT AND INTERNATIONAL SECURITY

After India conducted its nuclear explosive tests in May 1998, its nuclear weapons policy can be encapsulated as follows:

— India's security interests require the maintenance of an effective and credible minimum deterrent. This flows from the principle of minimum sufficiency which precludes an arms race with anyone.

— India has made a formal commitment to no first use of nuclear weapons.

— India maintains a unilateral moratorium on explosive nuclear tests. It is now engaged in discussions with key interlocutors on a range of issues, including the CTBT.

— India is engaged in negotiations in the Conference on Disarmament on a treaty banning the production of fissile material for nuclear weapons or other nuclear explosive devices.

— India has an effective export control mechanism in place to prevent the unauthorised transfer of sensitive equipment, material and technologies. This mechanism is continuously refined and updated.

— India's nuclear deterrent is based on the principle of strict political and civilian control. Such control would be exercised through appropriate scientific, technological and military management of the nuclear assets of the country to prevent unauthorised or accidental use.

India's policy on disarmament and international security issues is predicated on certain fundamental principles that are based on a broad national consensus. These are:

1) The primary factor in India's security calculus is the supreme national interest of safeguarding the sovereignty, independence and territorial integrity of the country.
2) Global nuclear disarmament and elimination of nuclear weapons is an indispensable requirement for regional and global security and for genuine and durable non-proliferation.
3) Disarmament and non-proliferation cannot be addressed in a piecemeal manner in artificially defined regional compartments. The all-pervading threat arising from the possession of weapons of mass destruction can only be removed with a holistic and global approach to the problem.
4) International disarmament and non-proliferation treaties should be universal and non-discriminatory and must provide equal security for all.
5) The clandestine and illegal transfer or receipt of sensitive materials, equipment and technology by some countries should not be overlooked or condoned for the sake of political expediency.
6) There is a need for the international community to develop effective safeguards against the danger of sensitive materials and weapons of mass destruction falling in the hands of extremist and terrorist organisations by accident or by the acts of governments that support such organisations.

By ratifying the Chemical Weapons Convention (CWC), India has demonstrated its commitment to international disarmament treaties, which are non-discriminatory in character.

The implementation of all obligations assumed by India as an original state party to the convention and related activities has proceeded satisfactorily. India is a party to the 1972 Biological and Toxic Weapons Convention (BTWC).

India actively participated in the work of Ad Hoc Group of State Parties to the Convention in Geneva during 1998 to negotiate a protocol to the convention on the basis of the agreed mandate. India envisions the Fissile Material Cut-off Treaty within the overall context of its security imperatives and the broader goal of universal nuclear disarmament. A limited moratorium covering individual countries is completely unacceptable.

The proliferation of small arms to non-state actors, the qualitative improvement in the lethality of small arms in terms of the impact of high technology and their easy availability had drawn the attention of the international community to the problem of small arms proliferation. Apart from a deliberate transfer of small arms to parties involved in low intensity conflicts there is also a widespread clandestine movement of such arms in the international market.

The weapons recovered by Indian forces from terrorists and insurgents in Jammu and Kashmir alone, which are enough to equip regular army divisions, are indicative of the magnitude of the problem and the need to prevent the deliberate proliferation of such arms. The problem of curbing the indiscriminate use of anti-personnel landmines became an emotive issue with numerous countries and NGOs calling for their total ban. India believes that while the concerns expressed are justified on humanitarian grounds, a phased approach is desirable till such time as alternative technologies are developed.

Countries plagued by landmines do not have the necessary manufacturing capability and are usually importers of such devices. The focus should thus be on restricting access coupled with increased demining activity. The use of mines should be permitted for the long-term defence of borders, perimeters and peripheries of states.

NON-MILITARY CHALLENGES TO INDIA'S SECURITY

Militancy in regions of India by groups actively supported from across the border has vitiated the security environment in the country. Governments that support such militancy must be careful of the long-term repercussions of fostering terrorism as a potentially destabilising factor for social peace and stability within their own countries.

The international community also has to guard against the spectre of the diversion of weapons of mass destruction, sensitive materials and technology to non-state actors. India is alive to the danger of the use of instruments such as currency counterfeiting and drugs trafficking as non-military challenges to security. The overall level of militancy in Jammu and Kashmir continues to show a downward trend. The key characteristics of present day militancy are the increased dependence on alien mercenaries, targeted attacks on those who have eschewed militancy and other soft targets as well as determined efforts to ignite and fuel communal tensions.

During Foreign Secretary level talks in Islamabad in October 1998 Pakistan was unambiguously told that India was aware of Pakistan's active involvement in promoting terrorism in India and that India would use all means necessary to stamp out the scourge of terrorism and insurgency. Meanwhile, the revival of political activity in Jammu and Kashmir state, increasing disillusionment of the people with militancy, and effective operations of the security forces have been largely responsible for the improved situation.

In the north-eastern region, militant activities of the various insurgent and extremist groups and ethnic tensions have kept the security conditions disturbed in several areas. The networking amongst the various militant groups in the region, reliance on trans-border bases, continuous efforts to arouse separatist tendencies, projection of alleged human rights violations and the so-called neglect of the region are some of the important aspects of the militancy in the region. The ceasefire in the state of Nagaland, which was initially declared from August 1, 1997 for a period of 3 months, has been extended from time to time and was last extended for a period of one year with effect from August 1, 1998.

Pakistani agencies operating from Nepal continued to launch operations against India. Pakistan provides support to organisations such as Tehrikul-Mujahideen, Al-Umar and

Jammu & Kashmir Islamic Front. Another dimension to the security climate in the north-east is the number of ULFA and Bodo camps that have been set up on the borders of certain countries neighbouring India.

Countries bordering this area have a common stake in uprooting terrorism and violence from the region to enable the overall development and prosperity of the people. Non-military challenges to India's security also include the linked problems of drugs trafficking, terrorism and organised crime. India is located in the middle of two of the world's leading narcotics producing and exporting regions—North-West Pakistan and Afghanistan on one side and Myanmar on the other. The involvement of insurgent an criminal groups in the drug trade is especially worrisome.

ENERGY SECURITY

Energy security is particularly crucial to India for two main reasons: the country's dependence on the imports of fossil fuels and the physical proximity of the two energy rich areas of the Gulf and Central Asia where competitive access rivalries contain inherent tendencies towards conflict involving outside powers. Inspite of improvements in indigenous production, dependence of energy sources like crude, petroleum products or imports continued. India's energy security would need to take into account some or all of the following factors:

— Mutually beneficial arrangements with India's eastern neighbours as well as Nepal for long term energy exploitation and sharing.

— Protection of the energy infrastructure within the country from disruption by terrorists and militants.

— Energy cooperation and sharing arrangements only with countries whose actions do not undermine India's security and which have demonstrated a willingness to cooperate meaningfully with India.

— International transit of energy destined for India only through stable, secure and friendly countries where there is no danger of disruption of supplies by state and non-state actors for political ends.

— Taking carefully calibrated actions to insulate India from disruption of supplies from outside by greater domestic production and recourse to nuclear and non-conventional energy sources.
— Cooperating with other interested parties in protecting the sea-lanes of communication.
— Diversification of supply routes within India.
— Focused investments in maritime and naval assets to ensure adequate reach and endurance.
— Greater involvement in exploration projects overseas pertaining to oil and gas resources.

3

Organisation and Functions of the Defence Ministry

A military department was created in the supreme government of the East India Company at Calcutta in the year 1776. Its main function was to sift and record orders relating to the army passed in other departments. It also maintained a list of army personnel. Although headed by a separate Secretary to the Government from 1776 onwards, it continued to function for many years as a branch of the public department. The Charter Act of 1833 brought about a number of changes in its administrative set-up under the East India Company. The Secretariat was reorganised in four departments, including a Military Department, each headed by a Secretary to the Government. In 1864, the Military Accounts Departments of Bengal, Bombay and Madras Presidencies were merged with the Military Department. The aımy, however, continued to function as the presidency armies till April 1895, when they were unified into a single Indian army. For administrative convenience, it was divided into four Commands, *viz.*, Punjab (including the North-West Frontier), Bengal, (including Burma) Madras and Mumbai (including Sind, Quetta and Aden).

The supreme authority over the Indian army was vested in the Governor General-in-Council, subject to the control of the Crown, which was exercised by the Secretary of State for India. In the council, there were two members responsible for military affairs, one of whom was the military member, who supervised all administrative and financial matters while the other was the Commander-in-Chief who was responsible for all operational matters. After 1909, the Military Department was renamed as the Army Department and was redesignated as the Defence department in 1938. In 1947, the Defence department became the Ministry of Defence under a cabinet minister.

POST-INDEPENDENCE ORGANISATIONAL SET-UP AND FUNCTIONS

On August 15, 1947, each Service was placed under its own Commander-in-Chief. Under the Constitution, the Supreme Command of the Armed Forces vested in the President. In 1955, the title of Commander-in-Chief was abolished and the three Service Chiefs were designated as the Chief of the Army Staff, the Chief of the Naval Staff and the Chief of the Air Staff, respectively.

In November 1962, a Department of Defence Production was set up to deal with research, development and production of defence equipment. The Department of Defence Supplies was created in November 1965 for planning and execution of schemes for substitution of import requirements for defence purposes. These two departments were later merged to form the Department of Defence Production and Supplies. A Scientific Adviser to the Defence Minister was appointed to advise him on scientific aspects of military equipment, research and design of equipment used by the defence forces. A Department of Defence Research and Development was created in 1980.

The Government of India is responsible for ensuring the defence of India and every part thereof. The responsibility for national defence rests with the cabinet. This is discharged through the Ministry of Defence, which provides the policy framework, and wherewithal to the armed forces to discharge their responsibilities in the context of the defence of the country. The Defence Minister is the head of the Ministry of Defence.

DEPARTMENTS

The Defence Secretary functions as head of the department of defence and is additionally responsible for coordinating the activities of the three departments in the ministry. The principal functions of the departments are as follows:

a) The Department of Defence deals with the three services and with inter-services organisations. It is also responsible for the defence budget, establishment matters, defence policy, matters relating to parliament, defence cooperation with foreign countries and coordination of all activities.

b) The Department of Defence Production and Supplies is headed by a Secretary and deals with matters pertaining to defence production, indigenisation of imported stores, equipment and spares, planning and control of departmental production units of the Ordnance Factory Board, and for Defence Public Sector Undertakings (DPSUs).

c) The Department of Defence Research and Development is headed by a Secretary, who is also the Scientific Adviser to the Defence Minister. It's function is to advise the government on scientific aspects of military equipment and logistics and the formulation of research, design and development plans for equipment used by the services.

The Finance Division of the Ministry of Defence is headed by a Financial Adviser. He is tasked with exercising financial control over proposals involving expenditure from the defence budget, and with the responsibility for internal audit and accounting of defence expenditure. In the latter tasks, he is assisted by the Controller General of Defence Accounts (CGDA).

COMMITTEES

A number of committees dealing with defence-related activities assist the Defence Minister. He holds weekly meetings which are attended by the Defence Secretary, Secretary (Defence Production and Supplies), Scientific Adviser to the Defence Minister, the Financial Adviser, Principal Secretary to the Prime Minister, Cabinet Secretary, Foreign Secretary and the Chiefs of Staff of the three services to review important developments and discuss issues concerning national security. The Raksha Mantri also chairs monthly meetings of the Defence Minister's Committee with the Secretaries in the Defence Ministry, Financial Adviser and the Chiefs of Staff of the three services to review and take coordinated decisions on various key programmes. The Chiefs of Staff Committee is a forum in which the service chiefs discuss matters having a bearing on the activities of the services and advise the ministry. The position of Chairman of the Chiefs of Staff Committee devolves on the longest serving Chief of Staff, and consequently rotates amongst the three services. To facilitate the task of the Chiefs of Staff Committee, a number of sub-committees have been set up.

The principal task of the Defence Ministry is to obtain policy directions of the government on all defence and security-related matters and communicate them for implementation to the Services Headquarters, Inter-Services Organisations, Production Establishments and Research and Development Organisations. It is also required to ensure effective implementation of the government's policy directions and the execution of approved programmes within the allocated resources.

The three Services Headquarters, *viz.*, the Army Headquarters, the Naval Headquarters and the Air Headquarters, function under the Chief of the Army Staff (COAS), the Chief of the Naval Staff (CNS) and the Chief of the Air Staff (CAS), respectively. They are assisted by their Principal Staff Officers (PSOs). The Inter-Services Organisations, under the Department of Defence, are responsible for carrying out tasks related to common needs of the three services like medical care, public relations and personnel management of civilians in the defence headquarters.

PLANNING FOR DEFENCE

The defence policy accommodates continuing changes in the strategic setting whilst ensuring that the armed forces deployed are well-equipped, properly manned and supported to allow them to undertake operations effectively. It is equally necessary to ensure that they are capable of responding to future challenges. The force structure is designed to provide a robust response to the new strategic environment whilst remaining sufficiently responsive to further development.

Systematic planning for effective implementation of the defence strategy and the security policy is the essence of planning for defence. The strategic and technological environment assessment based on the harmonised perception of experts, from all the concerned ministries and departments forms the basis for evolving the strategy. Planning for defence is a multidisciplinary exercise involving, inter alia, an assessment and understanding of the trends in the international security environment, foreign policy, economic and international relations and the internal security environment.

The Directorate General of Defence Planning Staff (DPS), an inter-service organisation, provides inputs to the Chiefs of Staff committee in charge of Defence Planning. The DPS is designed to be a multi-disciplinary group with representation from the three services, Defence, Finance, the Ministry of External Affairs and the DRDO. For sectoral planning, independent units function in the services headquarters which, in turn, are supported by the Departments of Defence, Defence Production and Supplies and Defence Research and Development.

DEFENCE EXPENDITURE

Given India's size and security concerns, the outlay on defence, assessed either as a percentage of the total central government expenditure or of the gross domestic-product, continues to be one of the lowest amongst neighbouring countries. The two charts in this chapter represent service/department-wise break up of defence expenditure for the years 1996-97, 1997-98, 1998-99 (RE) and 1999-2000(BE) and service/department-wise expenditure as a percentage of total defence expenditure.

4

The Indian Army

The basic responsibility of the army is to safeguard the territorial integrity of the nation against external aggression. Due to the country's long borders encompassing different geographical and climatic conditions, such as desert terrain on the west, snow-covered mountains in the north and thick rainfed mountainous jungles in the east, the army has to constantly prepare itself for diverse challenges. In addition, the army is often required to assist the civil administration during internal security disturbances and in the maintenance of law and order, in organising relief operations during natural calamities, like floods, earthquakes and cyclones and in the maintenance of essential services. Demands on the army have increased manifold due to continuous deployment of its forces in intense counter insurgency operations in Jammu & Kashmir and the north- east parts of the country. To achieve these objectives, the army has to be constantly modernised, suitably structured, equipped and trained.

Information Technology (IT) Activities

Major IT Projects under Implementation, Planning and Initiation are as under:-

a) *Replacement of Mainframe Computer*: The obsolete mainframe computer of 1983 vintage at Army Headquarters Computer Centre has been replaced with a high-end server RS-6000 of IBM.

(b) *Army Intranet*: Local Area Networks (LANs) at Army Headquarters (HQs) have been established. The Wide

Area Network (WAN) connectivity is under implementation to connect all HQs. With this connectivity, the flow of data and information with these HQs and within the HQs will improve manifold.

(c) *Automation of Research & Referral (R&R) Hospital*: The project for automation of the prestigious R&R Hospital, Delhi Cantt, is under consideration.

(d) *Automation of Record Offices (Phase V)*: Automation of the remaining 17 record offices had been taken up during the year.

(e) *Automation of Indian Military Academy (IMA)*: The case for full automation of IMA, Dehradun, has been initiated.

(f) *Pilot Project for Automation of a Corps*: A pilot project to evaluate the total automation requirements of a Corps, including headquarters in the chain (corps, divisions and brigades) and the units has been initiated. This pilot project will form the basis for automation of all the Corps of the army.

(g) *Enhancement of LAN at Command Headquarters*: The project will enhance the present limited capacity at command headquarters for meeting their full-networked management Information System (MIS) requirements. The case has been initiated during the current year.

MECHANISED FORCES

With a view to enhancing combat efficiency of the army, the following measures have been taken:

a) The Defence Research Development Organisation (DRDO) has developed an indigenous Main Battle Tank (MBT) *Arjun*, which will be the mainstay of the Indian army during the 21st century. Clearance has been accorded for production of tanks.

b) Import of T 90 S tanks from Russia has been approved.

c) Contract for Armoured Fighting Vehicle (AFV) radio sets is likely to be concluded.

d) FLAME anti-tank guided missile launchers are under the process of being delivered.

(e) The scheme for modernisation of T-72 tanks is under active consideration.

ARTILLERY

For meeting the urgent requirement of the Artillery, import of 155 mm smoke ammunition has been cleared and the same is likely to be delivered shortly. Battle Field Surveillance Radar (Medium Range) [BFSR (MR)] and Thermal Integrated Observation Equipment (IOE) have been contracted for and would be available to troops in the near future. Action has been initiated for procuring Weapon Locating Radar (WLR) in limited quantity ex-import.

INFANTRY

In order to provide mobility and protection to own troops against improvised explosive devices, the Mine Protected Vehicle is being acquired. A contract has been signed and the first consignment of few vehicles is expected to be despatched shortly. Snow mobiles have been procured and moved for use in the Siachen area. These will considerably ease out acute logistic problems of troops in the Siachen area. The supply order for 5.56 mm Light Machine Gun (LMG) & Passive Night Sight (PNS) for 5.56 mm Rifles/LMG has been placed with various vendors.

SIGNALS

During the year, significant development work has been done on some of the most critical equipment/ subsystem of Plan AREN.

a) *Automatic Electronic Switch (AES MK-II):* This has been developed as a product improvement of AES MK-I already in service. All evaluations of AES MK-II have been completed. The Bulk Production Clearance (BPC) is likely to be granted shortly.

b) *Radio Local System (RLS):* This system comprises one Radio Local Centre (RLC) and upto ten Radio Local Extensions (RLE). The equipment is used in fluid and mobile operations when paucity of time does not permit laying of field cables. The system integrates RLE subscribers into the Army Radio Engineering Network (AREN) grid. The RLSs have also been inducted.

c) *Radio Frequency 'F' (RRF) type:* This electronic counter measure (ECCM) fortified Frequency Hopping Radio Relay Set was introduced in June, 1998. The RRF will be subsequently upgraded.

e) *Trial and evaluation:* Trials and evaluation have been completed in respect of the following equipment:

(a) Fibre Optic Cable System (FOCS).

(b) Army Radio Engineering Network—Army Static Communication Network (AREN-ASCON) Pipeline Interface Unit (AAPIU).

(c) Radio Set HX.

ARMY AVIATION

Limited series production of Advanced Light Helicopter (ALH) is progressing and likely to be delivered during 1999. Emergency Locator Transmitter, Personnel Locator Beacon and homers have been contracted for.

ENGINEERS

Logistic upgradation in Siachen

Due to extremely low temperatures obtaining in the Siachen glacier area, disposal of night soil poses a great problem and leads to organic pollution. In order to preserve the delicate ecological balance of the Himalayas, bio-digesters were tried out for disposal of human waste through biodegradation. After successful trials at the base camp, the bio-digester has been recently installed at the glacier.

Pipeline project in Siachen

Kerosene oil is the basic necessity for troops deployed on the glacier. It is the primary fuel used for warming and cooking purposes. A major portion of the stores being air dropped is kerosene. A pilot project to pump kerosene oil using pipelines was executed to ascertain its feasibility and efficacy. The pilot project has performed well and the pipeline network is being extended to other locations on the glacier.

New mine field breaching systems

New minefield breaching system in the form of Engineer Mine Plough has been imported.

Army capital works

The management of Army Capital Works has been streamlined over the years. Close monitoring and careful cost control have resulted in most of the high value projects being completed on schedule and within the estimated cost. Completion of ongoing works continued to get priority to achieve an optimum use of the available resources and minimise cost overruns. Modern construction techniques and materials are being instituted gradually. The allocation of funds for capital works for the army during the financial year 1998-99 Rs. 438.80 crore which include Rs. 4,000 crore for special married accommodation under Quick Shelter Project initiated to achieve enhanced satisfaction levels of married accommodation. The emphasis continues on the construction of married accommodation expeditiously in a time-bound manner. Towards achieving this end, all married accommodation projects are being treated as fast track projects and works amounting to Rs. 16.32 crore have been sanctioned during 1998-99. During 1997-98, married accommodation comprising 729 units for officers, 571 units for JCOs and 3,301 units for OR have been completed.

Revenue works

The allocation of funds for revenue works and maintenance services is Rs. 114581 crore during 1998-99. To optimise the use of the available funds and to achieve higher users satisfaction, innovative schemes like door-to-door maintenance, welcome maintenance and single window system for attending to maintenance problems introduced earlier have been given a major thrust.

Completed works

A few important time-bound projects completed during 1997-98 and 1998-99 are given below:

a) Provision of Other Than Married (OTM) accommodation for a medium regiment at Jodhpur.

b) Project Quick Shelter (Phase-I) in 39 out of 42 high pressure stations.

c) Single officers accommodation for 164 officers at Mhow.

d) Provision of accommodation for two air observation post flights and base facilities for Army Aviation BMC at jodhpur.

e) Introduction of pre-fabricated construction of married accommodation at Gurgaon.

f) Infrastructural work for international Aerospace Exhibition 98 at Yelahanka, Bangalore.

g) Construction of building for Controller of Defence Accounts (CDA) (Navy) in Mumbai.

h) Augmentation of accommodation for naval hospital, Powai.

ELECTRICAL AND MECHANICAL ENGINEERS (EME)

The Corps of EME has dynamically moulded itself to keep pace with technological advancement in warlike equipment in providing engineering support to the equipment deployed across all the frontiers.

Simulators

EME has actively associated itself in the design, development and manufacture of simulators for imparting cost-effective and realistic training to the field army. The following simulators have been developed:

a) 'B' Veh Driving Simulators.

b) Hand Grenade Simulators.

c) Anti Tank Guided Missile (ATGM) Simulators.

Total quality management (TQM)

Development and training of EME officers and personnel were given a fresh impetus at the Military College of Electrical & Mechanical Engineering (MCEME), Secunderabad, which led to the institution being awarded ISO - 9001 and Golden Peacock National Training Award for excellence in training. Achieving yet another milestone in the field of TQM, 510 and 512 Army Base Workshops have been awarded ISO-9002 for excellence in technical output.

Overhaul/reoptimisation

In order to meet the challenges posed by changes in the international situation since 1991 and the recent United

States (US) sanctions, the Corps of EME has resorted to medium repair/overhaul/ reoptimisation of critical equipment such as T-72 tanks, BMP, Air Defence Weapon Systems, missiles, radars and communication equipment. Base workshops have also been geared up with modern CNC machinery for manufacture of selected spares of foreign origin.

Environmental protection

The corps of EME has contributed towards environmental protection and pollution control. EME has been entrusted with the implementation of pollution norms for military vehicles and equipment. It has been instrumental in establishing pollution check centres in major cities and identifying old vintage vehicles for transfer from metros to other cities.

Product improvement

The following product improvements are in an advanced stage of implementation:

a) Modification of Power Supply of Radar Cymbeline.

b) Modification of Audio Amplifier with Radio Sets ANPRC/ VC.

c) Modification of Alternator Circuit of Position and Azimutch Determining System (PADS) MK II.

d) Modification Fuel Injection Pump (FIP) Solenoid of Tank Vijayanta.

e) Fitting UTD-20 engines in BAZ 5937 (CV) and 5939 (TLV) of OSA AK weapon system.

f) Modification of the emergency gear controller of Vijayanta tank.

TERRITORIAL ARMY (TA)

The year was eventful due to heavy commitments of the units on embodiment of TA infantry units for 'Operation Rakshak' (Jammu & Kashmir) and security, guard/escort duties.

Ecological task forces

The Ecological Task Force (ETF) remained embodied for

eight months. The ETFs have performed commendably in greening the limestone quarries scarred hills around Mussoorie in Dehradun district, carry out plantation and greening in Garhwal district, the foothills of Samba in Jammu, greening around the desert in Jaisalmer district in Rajasthan, soil conservation and plantation in Chambal ravines in Morena district of Madhya Pradesh.

Non-departmental units

These are infantry units which are financed entirely by the Ministry of Defence. During the year, some of these infantry battalions remained embodied for internal security duties in 'Operation Rakshak' in J&K for tasks, such as guarding of vulnerable areas and points, manning permanent vehicle checkposts, road opening, convoy protection, cordon and search operations and detection of improvised explosive devices (IEDs). A few battalions were employed for guarding ASCON installations, Ordnance Depots, and Border Roads Organisation (in Doda J&K, Tripura, and Manipur areas). In addition some battalions were deployed for election duties in north-east during February to April, 1998.

REAMOUNT VETERINARY CORPS (RVC)

Raising of dog unit

Trained army dogs of the Indian army have acted as force multipliers when deployed with the security forces in combating insurgency in northern and eastern sectors. Their successful deployment has yielded commendable results which have been highly appreciated. Accordingly, government has accorded approval for raising of more dog units which has already commenced.

The government of India has gifted 8 trained dogs to the government of Bangladesh, which have been procured and trained by the Remount and Veterinary Corps of the Indian army. Bangladesh army personnel were also trained in handling and deploying the trained dogs. Army is selling surplus animals to paramilitary forces, state police, state governments and friendly foreign countries. This has led to generation of revenue worth Rs. 71,52,950 for the year 1997-98.

Under the Civic Aid Programme, RVC is regularly conducting Veterinary Aid Camps and Area Breeding programmes by providing free services of horse stallions, especially in Northern and Eastern Commands. The Veterinary Aid Camps provide free consultancy and treatment facilities to sick animals of civilians living in remote and farflung areas. The local population is also advised about the latest animal husbandry practices, prevention and control of animal diseases and knowhow to start poultry, sheep, goat and cattle-breeding projects. Veterinary Aid Camps have become a very useful tool in the hands of formation commanders for effective fraternisation of border population. Army dogs were deployed to fortify security arrangements along the route traversed by the pilgrims for Amarnath Yatra. Timely detection of IEDs by the army dogs have not only saved the lives of many pilgrims but also thwarted an attempt of the saboteurs, thus enhancing the image of the army in the minds of the people of the country.

UN PEACEKEEPING OPERATIONS

The Indian army is actively involved in the peacekeeping operation in Angola, Sierra Leone, Lebanon, Kuwait and Bosnia Herzegovina. Our troops with their professional approach and respect for human rights have earned respect from various non-government organisations and other UN agencies. One battalion group has taken over responsibilities as United Nations Interim Force in Lebanon (UNIFIL) from a Norwegian Battalion in Lebanon as of November 27, 1998.

The Rashtriya Rifles, under the operational control of the army, remained fully committed in counter-insurgency operations and have acquitted themselves creditably in the assigned role. A number of civic action programmes were conducted in the deployment areas in an attempt to mitigate the hardship faced by the people due to ongoing insurgency. Because of their valour and devotion to duty, 156 Rashtriya Rifles personnel have been awarded honours and awards during the period. A total of 96 Rashtriya Rifles personnel (7 officers, 3 JCOs and 86 other ranks) laid down their lives during the year in the service of the nation.

RECRUITMENT OF PERSONNEL IN THE ARMED FORCES

The New Recruitment System was introduced on April 1, 1998 in order to make recruitment more transparent, accessible to the public and to eradicate exploitation of candidates by touts and agents. The recruitment is carried out through rallies in order to reach out to the prospective candidates in the districts and far flung/remote areas. Relaxation has been given to wards of servicemen/ ex-servicemen/war widows in physical measurements and they are also awarded 20 per cent bonus marks on passing the written examination. Provision of instant enrolment has also been made for sons of battle casualties.

The intake of cadets in the National Defence Academy, Indian Military Academy and Officers Training Academy has shown a marked improvement. This trend, if continued, will arrest the deficiency in the officers category of the army in the next ten years and bring it within manageable proportions. With a view to providing opportunities to aspirants from within the ranks of the army and outside, a number of new entries like the Special Commissioned Officers Entry (for service entries), 10+2 entry, University Entry Scheme (Technical Graduates) and NCC Special Entry Scheme have been introduced.

The Women Special Entry Scheme has attracted a number of applications from potential women candidates for the Non-technical and judicial streams. The scheme has also been extended to widows of service officers killed in action. So far four widows have been commissioned into the army during 1998. Vacancy capacity per course is 50 with an annual intake of 100.

An Image Projection Campaign on mass media through TV, print and Radio was conducted by the army with the assistance of a professional advertising agency. This campaign has been received very well by the target audience. The positive effect of the campaign is apparent by way of improved intake in the training academics.

5

The Indian Navy

India is a maritime nation strategically straddling the Indian Ocean, with a substantive seaborne trade. The country's economic well-being is thus very closely linked to our ability to keep our sea-lanes free and open at all times. Besides, India has other maritime interests as well. Our island territories situated on our western and eastern seaboards are at considerable distances away from the mainland. To ensure their sustained development, umbilical linkages with the mainland and maritime security protection are essential prerequisites of our maritime security.

Our offshore assets within the Exclusive Economic Zone (EEZ) of 2.02 million sq.kms, fisheries and deep sea interests, major and minor harbours and the overall seaward security of long coastline and island territories are other vital aspects of our maritime dimension and the navy's responsibilities. Indian navy has consciously taken the difficult route of indigenisation in consonance with the national endeavour towards self-reliance. The navy embarked upon a programme for indigenous construction of ships and development of major subsystems, sensors and weapon systems with the help of Defence Research and Development Organisation (DRDO) and Defence Public Sector Understandings (PSUs).

Commissioning of the indigenously built destroyer, *INS Delhi* on November 15, 1997, with two more of the class in the pipeline along with other frontline ships under construction at the government shipyards have enabled the navy to become a builder's navy and not just be a buyer's navy. Self-reliance through indigenisation has been the navy's guiding philosophy over the last half century.

OPERATIONS AND ACTIVITIES

In its quest to maintain the highest level of vigil across the country's maritime boundary, the navy conducted various activities during the year.

Fleet exercises

Naval ships conducted regular tactical exercises, including amphibious landings, involving the three services and the coast guard. Both the current and new doctrines were rehearsed.

Surveillance patrol

Naval ships, submarines and aircraft maintained continuous surveillance off the coasts of Maharashtra, Saurashtra and Orissa, as also in the Palk Bay, to prevent smuggling of arms, drug trafficking and illegal movement of personnel. Naval forces successfully undertook major operations in the Andaman sea against gunrunners and narcotic dealers and apprehended a number of militants alongwith large catches of arms and ammunition. Some of the major operations were:

SNo	Operation	Duration	Units Participated
a)	"Leech"	Feb 09-11, 1998	Vindhyagiri, Saryu, Two LCUs, CGS Vivek, Lakshmibai, Islanders, CG Dornier Elements from 3 Madras, 5 X MI-8 Helicopters
b)	"Poorab"	May 29 to June 02, 1998	Saryu, Kuthar, LCU Islander, Dornier, Kirpan, 34, 35 CG
c)	"Hibiscus"	Aug 09-17, 1998	Khanjar, Himgiri, Saryu Kuthar.

Joint exercises with foreign navies

The Indian navy carried out joint exercises with naval units from Oman, Saudi Arabia, Kuwait, Iran, Mauritius, Seychelles, Maldives, Singapore, Vietnam, Philippines and United Kingdom. The units conducted Search and Rescue (SAR) exercises and other basic level exercises. Such interactions serve as good Confidence Building Measures (CBMs) and help foster friendly relations with these countries. These opportunities also provide a forum for disseminating the navy's, as also the country's, perceptions and policies on issues of interest to other countries.

NEW ACQUISITIONS

INS Kora, the first of the four missile corvettes being constructed indigenously at M/s Garden Reach Shipbuilders and Engineers Ltd (GRSE), Calcutta, was commissioned on August 10, 1998. Amongst the other acquisitions, an Extra Fast Attack Craft, INFACT-80, was commissioned on June 24, 1998. The second ship of the class joined the Indian navy by early 1999. The first indigenous Fleet Tanker, '*Aditya*' is in its final stages of construction at M/s GRSE, Calcutta, and is likely to be handed over to the Indian Navy (IN) by end of 1999 alongwith a Fast Attack Craft (under construction at M/s Goa Shipyard Ltd.).

The government has approved indigenous construction of two submarines and three frigates as also the acquisition of three frigates and two submarines from Russia. Of the two, one submarine was delivered to the Indian navy in December 1997. The Government has also approved modernisation of the aircraft carrier INS Viraat which commenced in May 1999.

After rendering yeoman service, the following ships would be decommissioned during 1999:

a) *INS Androth* and *Amala*
b) *INS Mesh* and *IN LCU L-31*
c) *INS Kesari*

COOPERATION WITH FOREIGN COUNTRIES

With the end of the cold war, international relations have undergone radical changes affecting the world order. This has necessitated most countries to forego their traditional confrontationist approach and seek new strategic alliances with the dual aim of promoting regional stability as also to progress towards the economic well-being of the nation state. Various international maritime cooperation initiatives by the Indian navy over the last few years have helped in building bridges with foreign navies which would go a long way in establishing a strategic relationship, based on mutual trust and confidence.

During the year, Indian Navy (IN) ships visited ports in Oman, Saudi Arabia, Iran, Mauritius, Seychelles, Maldives, Vietnam, Singapore, Malaysia, Philippines, South Korea, UAE and Bahrain. In addition, warships of most neighbouring countries in the Indian Ocean Region, as also ships from Italy, France and England visited Indian ports.

Exchange visits by high ranking defence officials help in strengthening the existing defence ties with other countries. the following senior naval dignitaries visited India during the year 1998:

a) C-in-C Russian Navy - January
b) Chief of Staff, Japanese MSDF - February
c) Chief of Staff, French Armed Forces - February
d) CNS Bangladesh Navy - March
e) Chief of General Staff, Polish Armed Forces - March
f) C-in-C Royal Thai Navy - April
g) Chief of General Staff, PLA of China - April
h) CNS Singapore Navy - July
i) CNS South African Navy - October
j) CNS Nigerian Navy - October

To meet the varied and multidimensional training requirements of foreign naval personnel, the Indian navy has well established institutions/academies imparting both basic and specialist training. These institutions are adequately geared up to meet the training requirements of friendly countries. Training to foreign nationals is imparted under various schemes, namely, International Technical and Economic Cooperation (ITEC) Programme, the Special Aid Scheme and the Self Financing Schemes (SFS). During the year 1997-98, 94 officers and 131 sailors from foreign navies were trained in India. A total of 345 vacancies was provided for training foreign nationals during the period 1998-99. The Indian navy hosts a regional congregation of the Navies (MILAN) of the littoral countries on a regular basis. These meetings are aimed to foster close ties between countries for developing confidence building in the region. The following MILANs were planned to be held in early 1999:

MILAN 99

A meeting of the Bay of Bengal littoral countries (MILAN 99) was hosted by the Indian navy at Port Blair in April 1999. MILAN 99 is planned as a sequel to 'MILAN 95' and 'MILAN 97' with a wider scope for interaction. Highlights of 'MILAN 99' include hosting of discussions on maritime subjects of mutual interests like Laws of the Sea, Pollution Control, Regional SAR and so on and presentation of papers on professional issues to promote regional security dialogues and Confidence Building Measures, joint exercises as also various sports/cultural activities.

Naval symposium

A naval symposium on 'Role of Navies in Littoral Warfare in the 21st century' was conducted by the Indian navy from February 3 to 7, 1999, at Kochi. Delegates from Sri Lanka, Maldives, UAE, Oman and Mauritius also participated in the symposium.

INDIGENOUS PROGRAMME

Significant strides have been made towards indigenisation of various equipment required by the Navy. R&D efforts by DRDO's chain of laboratories and the Weapons and Electronic Systems Engineering Establishment (WESEE) of the navy have been the mainstay in our efforts towards indigenisation of various equipment.

Weapon systems/spares

The acquisition, maintenance and product support of naval weapons and equipment used to be heavily dependent on foreign suppliers. In order to achieve better product support and move towards self reliance, the Indian navy has been promoting indigenisation of spares, sub systems and systems used on board naval ships, through domestic industry in the 420 private and public sectors. Some of the major projects under progress are:

a) Triple Tube Torpedo Launcher.

b) Super Rapid Gun Mount

c) Anti Missile System Trishul.

d) APARNA Radar

e) Electro Optical Fire Control System—EQN 51.

f) Sonar HUMSA.

g) Submarine Sonar Panchendriya.

Underwater ranges

The project for setting up of an underwater range at Goa for measurement of magnetic and noise signatures of naval platforms is in the advance stage of execution. On completion, the facility would enhance the operational effectiveness of naval ships and submarines, particularly for shallow water operations. The modernisation of the aircraft carrier *Viraat* commenced in India in May 1999. A major part of the onboard equipment is slated for replacement by indigenous equipment being supplied by Indian industries.

RF test range

The government has approved the setting up of a scale model RF test range at *INS Valsura* (Jamnagar). The range would provide facilities for undertaking scale model studies of ships in a simulated RF environment with a view to optimise ship design in achieving electromagnetic compatibility.

MAINTENANCE

The Indian navy is operating gas turbines for propulsion and power generation on board naval ships. These engines are in the range of 12-14 MW for propulsion and 900 KW for power generation. The centre would cater for overhauling and testing of the M15E and M36 gas turbines, which would be a major step towards self reliance. The only Floating Dock, FDN-1, with the navy is being refitted for the first time at M/S Hindustan Shipyard Ltd, Visakhapatnam.

The Naval Dockyard (Mumbai) has successfully undertaken rewinding and overhauling of a 1MW alternator in May 1998. Until now the dockyard had undertaken repairs of alternators upto 750 KW capacity.

DELEGATION OF FINANCIAL POWERS

A delegation of financial powers in the Navy, with the institutationalisation of 'New Management Strategy' (NMS) has resulted in greater efficiency in all field formations. The areas where the Navy has benefited the most on account of delegation of revenue powers are refit of ships, procurement of stores and training. The net gain has been in greater operational availability of ships, submarines and aircraft

In its quest to build upon the advantages, which have accrued through NMS, the Navy has automated its entire procurement process through creation of a WAN-Integrated Logistics Management Systems (ILMS). The navy has also achieved computerisation of its financial management requirement which is proposed to be linked with the Management Information System. The greatest fallout of the delegation of financial powers is that the navy today is more budget aware and expenditure is being prioritised to achieve the "best value for money".

HYDROGRAPHY

India, with its hydrographic traditions dating back to the 17th century, is the foremost hydrographic nation in the Indian Ocean region.

The National Hydrographic Department (NHD) compares favourably with all the major hydrographic countries in terms of resources and expertise. The National Hydrographic Department (NHD) is recognised as a regional leader for undertaking training as well as hydrographic surveys. The NHD has six indigenously designed and constructed survey ships fitted with the latest hydrographic instrumentation and equipment.

The ships are capable of 4-31 undertaking all types of survey assignments. Two more ships of the same class are under construction in an Indian shipyard and are likely to be delivered by A.D 2000-2001.

The NHD earned revenue for the navy during 1997-98 by undertaking contract surveys including coastal zone management surveys. The department is undertaking trials of the electronic navigational charts prepared by it as part of the programme to produce such charts for the entire area covering the Indian coast/waters. The department is also involved in surveys related to the continental shelf and baselines as per requirements of the UN convention on laws of the sea.

COMMERCIAL DIVING

The navy will conduct the following 'Commercial Diving Courses', on a payment basis:

a) Indian Diving Standards (IDS) I to IV courses.
b) Conversion Courses from one level to another within IDS.
c) Training of divers from commercial diving companies for undertaking specific diving tasks.
d) Specially tailored diving courses for personnel of police, port trusts, hydel projects, fire brigades and so on.

Personnel

The importance of creating the software and human resource base, which will anticipate as well as respond simultaneously to the changing technology, needs no further emphasis. Naval warfare, by nature, remains at the front end of high technology and therefore, requires continuous upgradation of the technological and innovative skills of its personnel. Towards this quest, the induction pattern, training facilities and methodologies at the training schools/ establishments and repair yards, as well as the on-job training on board ships and submarines has been constantly reviewed to adopt modern practices and enable seamless integration.

Women in all branches of the Indian Navy

Induction of women as Short Service Commission (SSC) officers in the support branches/cadres of the Indian navy commenced in 1992. Of these, 99 women officers have been inducted during the last six years in the education branch and law, logistic and air traffic controller cadres of the executive branch. The government has now approved induction of women, as SSC officers, in all branches of the Indian navy. Women technical graduates will also be able to join the operational cadres in the field of highly sophisticated propulsion machinery, weapons systems and sensors with a network of information technology. The Indian navy will be one of the very few navies in the world wherein women officers have been actively employed on board ships.

SPORTS AND ADVENTURE ACTIVITIES

Sports and adventure activities continued to play an

important part in naval life. The Navy Adventure Cell at Naval Headquarters organises various activities in the navy. During the year, hot air ballooning, rafting, trekking, powered hang gliding, para sailing, skydiving, wind surfing, kayaking, mountaineering and skiing were undertaken for naval personnel and their families.

Sky to ocean expedition

A multidisciplinary expedition from Indira Col (Saichen) to Indira Point (Andaman & Nicobar Islands) named "Sky to Ocean" was conducted by the army from August to November 1998. The expedition, encompassing 14 disciplines of adventure activities, was flagged off by the Defence Minister on September 3,1998 in New Delhi. The naval participation in this expedition was in the following disciplines:

a) Trekking, mountaineering and skiing.

b) Rowing/rafting.

c) Skydiving and hot air ballooning.

d) Motor cycle expedition.

e) Wind surfing.

f) Scuba diving.

International Achievements of Naval Sportsmen/Coaches

Naval sportsmen participated in various international fixtures and brought laurels to the country by winning medals in the various events. Participation by N.G Dingko, Petty Officer (Steward) and D. Wilson, Petty Officer (Steward) in boxing and weightlifting respectively at the Commonwealth Games—1998, in Malaysia are cases in point.

WELFARE

Various activities to improve community development in the navy as also its quality of life were initiated. Prevention of AIDS and family planning were accorded high priority. Other welfare measures instituted in the navy included the rehabilitation of widows, computer coaching classes, yoga training, protection of environment and so on. The Indian navy established a 'Naval Maritime Academy' (NAMAC) at Mumbai to conduct courses for retiring naval personnel/ children of service personnel interested in seeking employment in the Merchant navy. In addition, the Krendria Vidyalaya Sangathan has granted additional concessions, at the insistance of the navy, to ease problems faced by serving and retired defence personnel seeking admission of their wards to Kendriya Vidyalaya schools.

6

The Indian Air Force

The Indian Air Force (IAF) today, having completed more then six decades of dedicated service to the nation, is a modern, technology-intensive force distinguished by its commitment to excellence and professionalism.

Keeping pace with the demands of contemporary advancements, the IAF continues to modernise in a phased manner and today it stands as a credible air power as the nation marches into the next millennium. With the ever escalating costs of operations, great emphasis is being placed on cost-effective training, reducing expenditure, optimising output and minimising wastage.

The air force has implemented a number of measures to enhance the quality of life of its personnel in key welfare areas of housing, education and hostel facilities. In addition to the traditional wartime roles of the IAF of counter-air, counter-surface, strategic and combat support operations, the air force has provided significant aid to civil authorities during natural calamities like the Gujarat cyclone and the Malpa tragedy.

The Siachen glacier lifeline continues to be monitored by the Indian air force, fully supporting the Indian army in fighting on the world's highest battlefield.

The IAF has also provided aid to civil authorities for the large scale movement of military and paramilitary personnel to maintain law and order as well as to cater for the needs of a large number of airmen and jawans in remote and inaccessible outposts.

MODERNISATION

Air superiority today is a mandatory prerequisite to land and sea battle. Keeping in mind the acquisitions and capabilities of our potential adversaries, a continuous review of the state and performance of existing assets is indispensible.

Where cost factors do not permit replacements, indigenisation and mid-life updates have been selected as alternatives, extending the life and effectiveness of valuable and expensive aircraft over a larger span of time.

In some cases, the air force has upgraded the avionics and associated systems, while in others, it has inducted multi-role capability at minimal cost to the exchequer.

UPGRADE OF COMBAT AIRCRAFT

The upgrade of the MiG 21 Bis has commenced in earnest and those for the MiG 27 and Jaguar aircraft are on the anvil. This would provide a fresh lease of life to these fighters, maintaining them as a potent force till well into the next century.

The mid-life update on the MiG 21 Bis is going on as per schedule. Currently, two aircraft are in Russia for upgrade. The subsequent plan is to overhaul and upgrade the remaining aircraft at the Hindustan Aeronautics Ltd. (HAL).

ADVANCED JET TRAINER (AJT)

In the absence of an optimally designed advanced jet trainer, the IAF has inducted a large number of MiG 21 trainers to ensure continuity to the fighter pilot training programme on the MiG 21.

ELECTRONIC WELFARE SUPPORT SYSTEMS

Electronic Warfare Systems enhance survivability in a dense and lethal air defence environment. The IAF today has placed great emphasis on such systems and most aircraft are now equipped with state-of-the-art electronic systems for Radar Warning and Counter Measure Dispensing Systems to upgrade their survivability and enhance their operational effectiveness.

OPERATIONS

Air defence

The air defence of the nation is the foremost task of the IAF. To further strengthen its air defence shield, the IAF is continuously improving upon the performance of ground radars, their integration, automation of data transfer and displays. Combined with dedicated interceptors and guided missiles, the layered structure presents an effective and efficient air defence system.

Offensive strike capability

The IAF has a variety of multi-role and dedicated strike aircraft to present a formidable combat capability acting both as an effective deterrence against adventurism by our adversaries and to effect a crippling strike should the necessity arise. The SU-30 -multi-role air superiority fighter was formally inducted into the IAF last year. The aircraft and the aircrew are now operationally well prepared. With this acquisition, the IAF's strike as well as air defence capability have taken on a new dimension.

Operational training

The Indian air force has continued to carry out extensive operational training in the form of major air exercises both within own elements as well as extensive interaction in joint exercises with the army and the navy. New concepts, philosophies and tactics have been evolved to conform with the changing threat scenario. These elaborately planned, single as well as joint exercises have helped in improving our capabilities and fostering inter-service cooperation and jointmanship. Such joint exercises have been held in all the various terrain and climatic conditions obtaining in our environment both on land and over the sea. The exercises have constituted high points of the training activities for the year, ensure crew fitness and re-confirm our confidence in our capabilities.

SHIFTING OF HEADQUARTERS OF SOUTH WESTERN AIR COMMAND

The South Western Air Command shifted its headquarters. The move was conducted very fluently, without any break in the effective functioning of the headquarters during the change. The government of Gujarat extended all cooperation and support in facilitating the establishment of the headquarters at its new location.

DISPLAYS

The flying displays saw participation by frontline fighters including the highly agile SU-30 attired in the national tricolour performing most impressively. The original IAF aerobatic team called the 'Thunderbolts' equipped with the redoubtable Hunter aircraft were rested due training requirements of the air force. The IAF has revived its formation aerobatic team reinstated as the "Surya Kiran". Along with the skydiving team 'Akash Ganga' they have performed most professionally across the country. The National Golden Jubilee celebrations were enjoined befittingly by the air force by organising numerous static displays and flypasts at several cities throughout the country including Mumbai, Chennai, Cochin, Srinagar, Jodhpur, Lucknow and Visakhapatnam.

As an ongoing development of a comprehensive IT base, the IAF has initiated Project "Inventory Material Management On-Line System (IMMOLS)" to computerise its inventory. The project is well under progress. Operational and maintenance management activities are also being completed under project "Computerised Operations and Maintenance Management Package (COMMPACK)". On completion, the project would computerise the entire operations/maintenance/miscellaneous activities of flying bases and ground weapon systems and thus would lead to a total computerisation in the IAF.

ADMINISTRATION

The Indian air force has made significant progress in improving the quality of life of its personnel. Improving the quality and the numbers of dwelling units of residential accommodation has been a priority area for the air force. During the current financial year, the construction of an additional 2,600 dwelling units is planned.

FAMILY WELFARE

Prevention of AIDS and family planning continued to be high

priority areas. The air force has implemented the family welfare programme through seven Class I and 29 Class II welfare centres. Amongst a myriad of other welfare thrusts of the air force are the setting up of dental chairs, rehabilitation of widows of personnel losing their lives while still in harness, subsidy for dwelling units for widows, establishment of numerous computer awareness programmes and setting up of a marriage bureau.

ADVENTURE SPORTS

The momentum generated by IAF adventure activities during the Golden Jubilee celebrations last year continued into this year also. A highly successful and popular sequence of air shows continued with the Air Devils carrying out sky diving demonstrations at Port Blair, Lucknow, Mumbai, Chandigarh and Calcutta.

In addition, existing adventure activities such as mountaineering, water sports, horse riding, trekking, hang gliding were undertaken. The para sailing camp drew active participation by over 3,000 air force personnel. An adventure camp for Air Force school children at Mount Abu and Dalhousie drew enthusiastic response during the summer holidays.

SUPER SPECIALITY VETERANS' HOSPITAL

Currently there are certain serious diseases whose treatment is not authorised in service hospitals. In order to alleviate the suffering of retired air force personnel against such life-threatening situations, a Super Speciality Veterans' Hospital has been established in Delhi with facilities available for radiotherapy, haemodialysis. bronchoscopy and physiotherapy.

SENIOR CITIZENS INSTITUTE

An old age home for lonely retired air force personnel is under construction at Tughlakhabad, New Delhi. This care centre would have facilities like messing, canteen, clinic, dispensary, library and a physiotherapy centre located within the complex.

EDUCATIONAL PROGRAMMES

Ab-initio trainees are being given inputs in computer

education throughout the Indian air force. Advanced PCs have been procured and supplied to all training institutes of the IAF for widespread training in computer education.

FLIGHT SAFETY

The entire flight safety organisation in the IAF remained geared during the year to reducing flying accidents and conserving precious resources required to maintain high standards of operational preparedness at all times.

During the last two years, accidents due to human error and bird strike have shown a marked downward trend. The IAF, during 1996-97, recorded its lowest ever accident rate. This was repeated in 1997-98 and efforts are underway to reduce these figures even further. Some of the measures in this regard are:

Accident investigation

Each accident or incident is thoroughly investigated. Specialists from the Ministry of Defence and manufacturers are involved in Courts of Inquiry, as and when required. The recommendations made by these courts are implemented to avoid a recurrence.

COFAA

The Committee on Fighter Aircraft Accidents (COFAA) is a high powered committee, which was initially set up to monitor accidents on fighter aircraft. The scope of the committee was subsequently enlarged to cover accidents on other aircraft also. The recommendations of this committee are expected to go a long way in further enhancing flight safety in the IAF.

Bio-acoustic devices

Bio-Acoustic devices have been procured and installed for bird strike prevention on vulnerable airfields. These have been found to be effective. Regular monitoring of bird strike incidents is being carried out to check the efficacy of these aids. Zon guns are noise devices intended to scare birds. The Liquefied Petroleum Gas (LPG) fired zon guns have been procure and installed at some of the vulnerable airfields.

INSTITUTE OF FLIGHT SAFETY

The Institute of Flight Safety, the only one of its kind in

South Asia, trains officers and other personnel in accident investigation and prevention. It has been conducting regular courses for the IAF, Army, Navy, HAL and the Directorate General of Civil Aviation (DGCA). It is also engaged in research and analysis and publicity to build up flight safety awareness. During the beginning of the year, the Institute of Flight Safety conducted an International Flight Safety Seminar on Human Error Accidents. Delegates from over 40 countries attended and valuable lessons were drawn from the experiences of air forces the world over on human error accidents.

PREVENTION OF BIRD STRIKES

In order to reduce the probability of bird strikes to aircraft, it is proposed to sanitise 10 priority airfields within a radius of 10 km. A project report is being prepared on the subject by Housing & Urban Development Corporation (HUDCO). The Ministries of Agriculture, Urban Affairs and Dairying will install modern abattoirs, carcass utilisation plants and ensure general cleanliness in the sanctioned areas, which would go a long way in further enhancing the anti-bird programme of the air force. In addition, an environmental inspection of all airfields is being carried out to monitor the flight safety environment at each base. This obviously pays dividends in the accident/ incident prevention programmes at the airbases.

Flight safety zones have been created at all airfields as a bird strike prevention measure.

INDUCTION AND TRAINING (IAF)

Induction in officer cadre of IAF

Induction into the officers cadre of the Indian air force is done through:

a) Union Public Service Commission (UPSC).
   i) National Defence Academy (NDA) Examination
   ii) Combined Defence Services (CDS) Examination

b) Direct recruitment.

c) In-service recruitment.

A common entrance examination is held by the UPSC for NDA and CDS examinations, the syllabi for which is widely publicised and made known to all aspirants. All successful candidates based on the results of the written examination are sent to Air Force Selection Boards for further interviews and Officer Like Qualities (OLQ) tests.

The results of the Air Force Selection Board tests are announced openly immediately after the completion of the test at the Service Selection Boards.

Thereafter, recommended candidates are detailed for medical examinations. Whilst calling the candidates for Selection Board tests, complete details pertaining to the medical requirements are also intimated to them in writing so that they are aware of the medical fitness levels that would be required from them. The selection board marks are forwarded to the UPSC who finally release the merit list through newspapers.

In so far as direct recruitment is concerned, the advertisements giving complete details of the qualification requirements and other details are published in the *Employment News*, *Rozgar Bulletin* and leading national dailies at least one year in advance.

On receipt of applications, in response to the advertisements, the same are thoroughly, checked for eligibility and eligible candidates are subsequently called for Service Selection Board (SSB) interview.

The selection process at Service Selection Boards involves well publicised information which has been disseminated through books, magazines, brochures and even television programmes. The results of the SSB tests are openly announced.

In-service induction into the officers cadre is done through a widely publicised written examination. Those who qualify in the same are sent for Service Selection Board tests.

RECRUITMENT OF AIRMEN TO THE AIR FORCE

Recruitment of airmen is done through the Central Airmen Selection Board, New Delhi. There are thirteen selection centres spread all over India and they make necessary arrangements for the conduct of selection tests and final enrolment. After seeking applications through advertisements in national and regional dailies and through the mass media, a written test on an All India basis is held and an All India Merit List drawn up for purpose of recruitment. Enrolment is done in order of merit. Allocation of trades is done on the basis of Trade Allocation Tests. The number of personnel recruited varies as per requirement.

7

The Indian Coast Guard

The Indian Coast Guard (CG) was set up as an armed force of the union in 1978 on recommendations of Rustamji Committee for preservation and protection of our Exclusive Economic Zone (EEZ). The CG is responsible for keeping India's EEZ measuring over 2.02 million sq.kms. under regular surveillance in order to prevent poaching/smuggling and other illegal activities in the EEZ. Besides, the CG's charter of duties include pollution control at sea, search and rescue (SAR) and protection of marine environment.

The initial Coast Guard Development Plan (CGDP), 1978-90 (Kamath Plan) was reviewed in 1987 and a 15 year Perspective Plan (1985-2000) for the growth of CG upto the turn of the century was made. However, the CG plans had to be recast again to be coterminus with the National Development Plan 1992-97. The last Development Plan (CGDP 1992-97) envisaged acquisition of 30 ships and 30 aircraft but only 9 ships and 13 aircraft could be inducted into the service.

In the CGDP 1997-2002, it is proposed to acquire capabilities hitherto not available in the CG like pollution control vessel, hovercraft, indigenous Advance Light Helicopter (ALH) and Medium Range Surveillance aircraft (MRSA) besides patrol vessels as per details given below:

	Type	*Number*
a)	Fast patrol vessel	02
b)	Interceptor boats	02
c)	Pollution control vessel	04

d)	Advanced offshore patrol vessel	02
e)	Hovercraft	06
f)	MRSA	02
g)	Twin engine helicopters	02
h)	20 mm guns	23
i)	30 mm Guns	12

ORGANISATION

The command and control of the CG is exercised by the Director General, Coast Guard, New Delhi. It has three regional commands with the regional headquarters situated at Mumbai, Chennai and Port Blair. The entire coastline of India and the maritime zones are divided into three regions. The regions are further divided into 11 coast guard districts, each representing a coastal state, under a district Commander. There are two air stations at Daman and Chennai and four air enclaves at Goa, Mumbai, Calcutta and Port Blair.

FORCE LEVEL

From a small beginning in 1978, the CG has made rapid progress in developing its force levels with regular induction of ships and aircraft. Currently, the CG has a force level of 34 ships, 15 interceptor boats/crafts and 32 aircraft. One more ship is going to be inducted in the near future as the ship is in an advanced stage of construction.

OPERATIONS

In addition to the normal peacetime role of the CG comprising surveillance and patrol on EEZ, certain specific operations are also being undertaken to counter the threat of insurgency. These operations are detailed below:

Operation tasha

Consequent to the withdrawal of Indian Peace Keeping Force (IPKF) from Sri Lanka, protection of Tamil Nadu Coast against infiltration of militants was entrusted to the navy and CG. One CG ship is on patrol in the Palk Bay on task at all times. One IB/IC from Mandapam is also on patrol alongwith one Dornier aircraft for air surveillance. From April 1998 to February 17, 1999, the CG ships collectively were deployed for 402 days at sea while Coast Guard aircraft were on task for 325 hours for this operation.

Operation swan

In 1993, consequent to the Mumbai serial bomb blasts, large-scale smuggling of arms and explosives was reported from sea routes adjoining Maharashtra and Gujarat coasts. To counter this, in April 1993, Operation Swan was launched in coordination with the navy to patrol sensitive areas off the west coast. These operations contained the situation to a large extent. From April 1998 to February 17, 1999, the CG ships were deployed for 338 days at sea while CG aircraft were on task for 466.39 hours for this operation.

Operation "nakabandi"

With increased hostilities in Sri Lanka, influx of Tamil refugees recommenced. Local fishermen have started smuggling diesel and other explosive making material to aid Liberation Tigers of Tamil Eelam (LTTE). To check the influx of refugees and to curb the clandestine activities in Palk Bay and Gulf of Mannar, Operation "Nakabandi" was launched on August 13, 1996. From April 1998 to February 17, 1999, about 2,850 refugees belonging to 1,052 families were reported to have come to India. During this period, CG ships apprehended 7 Sri Lankan fishing boats with 38 crew members.

ANTI-SMUGGLING SEARCH & RESCUE (SAR) & OTHER OPERATIONS

The details of anti-smuggling, search and rescue and other operations are given below:

Anti-smuggling operations

The CG ships and aircraft carry out routine anti-smuggling patrol and apprehended contraband worth of Rs. 259.48 crore till February 1999.

Search and rescue operations (SAR)

During the period from April 1998 to February 17, 1999 CG ships and aircraft undertook 37 SAR missions and were instrumental in saving 129 lives at sea after receipt of distress messages from International Maritime Coordination

Centre (INMCC), Bangalore. This has strengthened the SAR responses in the Indian Ocean under the new Global Maritime Distress Safety System (GMDSS) operation. Till February 17, 1999 CG ships and aircraft undertook 695 sorties in response to distress messages and have saved 895 lives.

Security of offshore installations

CG ships and aircraft are deployed for patrolling the oil rigs on regular basis. The Director General of Coast Guard (DGCG) is the chairman of the offshore security coordination committee which discusses the security and disaster management of oil rigs once in a quarter.

Anti-poaching activity

During the current year, CG ships on patrol in the Indian EEZ apprehended 21 fishing trawlers with 188 crew engaged in illegal fishing without valid documents. Since its inception, the CG apprehended 607 foreign fishing vessels with crew. Regular patrolling by the CG in the Indian EEZ has acted as deterrence to poachers, although the number of ships available is still limited in relation to the total area to be kept under surveillance.

ASSISTANCE RENDERED

Fishing vessels

During the period under report, CG ships and aircraft assisted 11 fishing boats and 22 merchant ships in distress at sea. CG ships also carried out mid-sea repartriation as follows:

a) 43 Indian fishermen with 08 boats from Sri Lanka.
b) 20 Sri Lankan fishermen with 03 boats from India.
c) 190 Indian fishermen with 31 boats from Pakistan.
d) 149 Pakistani fishermen with 14 boats from India.

SECURITY

The details are as follows:

National data buoy programme of national institute of ocean technology

CG ships and aircraft are providing security for national

data buoys laid down in various positions in Arabian Sea and Bay of Bengal for collection and monitoring of oceanographic data by the Department of Ocean Development.

VVIPs seaward security

During the period under review, the CG ships and aircraft were deployed to provide seaward security to various dignitaries including the President and the Vice-President of India.

MANPOWER PLANNING, RECRUITMENT AND TRAINING

Basic training in the CG is provided at the Naval Training Establishments. Since April 1998 to February 17, 1999, the coast guard has recruited 30 officers including 5 Women Officers, 40 yantriks and 265 naviks. CG personnel are also deputed for reputed specialised courses like Staff Course at Defence Services Staff College (DSSC), Wellington, College of Defence Management (CDM), Secunderabad, and Naval Staff College, USA. Besides, for the last three years, CG pilots are being trained for the Basic Flying, Air Traffic Controller and Qualified Flying Instructor courses with the Indian Air Force.

POLLUTION RESPONSE

The coast guard is a primary agency for protection of maritime environment of India under the National Oil Spill Disaster Contingency Plan. So far the coast guard has undertaken about 36 oil spill operations. During the current year, CG ships and aircraft carried out two pollution response operations as per details given below:

(a) March 12, 1998 off Mumbai—Gas leakage off Mumbai harbour (Noble Jimmi Pucket)

(b) May 31, 1998—Oil spill of Vadinar (SDM)

NATIONAL INTEGRATION

The CG has been a true picture of a big family consisting of members from different religions and castes. CG personnel, recruited from various parts of the country, farflung areas and islands, are posted on board various ships/stations along the coast for carrying out the chartered duties of the service. Cooperation, sense of belonging and brotherhood are the essence of this efficient and motivated service, where they portray the true picture of national integration.

COOPERATION BETWEEN COAST GUARD AND CIVIL AUTHORITIES

Evacuation of patient

On May 18, 1998, CGS Varuna evacuated one patient from MV Scan Palaris who was admitted in Trust Hospital, Kochi, after giving first aid.

Aid to kandla port authority

From June 11 to 30, 1998, *CGS Veera* was deployed in Gulf of Kutch/Kandla for SAR operations after the cyclone hit Kandla Port. The helicopters launched from the ship carried out sorties to locate dead bodies and also assisted in transporting men and material from the grounded ships. The ship *Gemini* was also utilised in search and transportation of dead bodies, and so on from the sea to harbour.

Food dropping in tribal areas of A&N island

On February 14 and 23, March 12 and May 13,1998, CG Dornier carried out sorties for dropping food in tribal areas of Island.

8
Defence Production

The department of defence production was set up in 1962, in the aftermath of the Chinese aggression to create an indigenous defence production base which is self-reliant and self-sufficient. Indigenisation, particularly of armaments, proceeded apace in 1963. In November 1965, the Department of Defence Supplies was created to forge linkages between the civil industries and defence production units. The two departments were merged in December 1984 to form the Department of Defence Production and Supplies.

Since 1962, 16 new ordnance factories have been set up and their capacities have been augmented and modernised selectively keeping in mind the emerging requirements of the armed forces. Presently, 39 ordnance factories and 8 Defence Public Sector Undertakings (DPSUs) are engaged in the task of manufacture of equipment and stores for defence services. In addition, capacities of civil sectors are also utilised for the purpose. The DPSUs are:

i) Hindustan Aeronautics Limited (HAL)
ii) Bharat Electronics Limited (BEL)
iii) Bharat Earth Movers Limited (BEML)
iv) Mazagon Dock Ltd. (MDL)
v) Goa Shipyard Limited (GSL)
vi) Garden Reach Ship builders and Engineers Limited (GRSE)
vii) Bharat Dynamics Limited (BDL)
viii) Mishra Dhatu Nigam Limited (MIDHANI)

The following organisations are also associated with the Department of Defence Production and Supplies for technical support:

i) Directorate General of Quality Assurance (DGQA)

ii) Directorate General of Aeronautical Quality Assurance (DGAQA)

ii) Directorate of Standardisation

iv) Directorate of Planning and Coordination

v) Defence Exhibition Organisation (DEO)

These defence production units have become increasingly self-reliant. Additional capacities have been created and new items have been productionised. These include the main battle tank *Arjun*, the Advanced Light Helicopter (ALH) and a range of 155 mm antitank ammunition.

The defence sector corporates lend diversity, operational flexibility and enhanced efficacy borne out of autonomy and commercial disposition. The ordnance factories and the DPSUs are to make use of civil and export sector in order to enhance the viability without detracting from defence commitments. These measures forge interaction between the defence production sector and civil industry to contribute to steady growth in the overall turnover of these units.

The total value of sales by ordnance factories and defence public sector undertakings is as follows:

(Rupees in crore)

Year	*Ordnance Factories Total Sales*	*PSUs Sales*
1996-97	2597.00	5167.17
1997-98	3071.00	6063.10
1998-99 (Targets)	3938.00	7104.00
1998-99 (Achievements (Prov.) up to Dec. 98)	2155.00	2855.00

The defence public sector undertakings and the ordnance factories have made exports of Rs. 76 crore as against the target of Rs. 189 crore for the year 1998-99. Thirty-eight out of 39 ordnance factories, all the manufacturing units of HAL, BEML, MIDHANI, all divisions/units of BEL, production division in BDL and 3 units of GRSE have been awarded ISO 9002 series of certification.

In order to project fully Indian capabilities in aeronautics, the Department of Defence Production and Supplies through Hindustan Aeronautics Limited (HAL) and in association with the Defence Research and Development Organisation, the Department of Space, the Department of Civil Aviation, and the Indian Air Force, organised the second international Aero Space Exposition—'Aero India 1998' at Yelahanka Air Base Bangalore from December 8 to 12, 1998. The exposition was inaugurated by the Defence Minister. Delegations from 17 countries visited the air show and about 110 international and 62 national companies participated in this event.

The activities of the organisations, under the Department of Defence Production and Supplies are given in the succeeding paragraphs.

SUPPLIES WING

The Supplies Wing is responsible for locating and developing broadbased indigenous supply sources, public and private, for defence equipment. Accordingly, the main functions of Supplies Wing are:

a) Identification of imported items for indigenous development with industry;

b) Organising production of imported items developed by the DRDO in the civil sector; and

c) Functioning as the nodal agency, in the Ministry of Defence for evolving purchase policies.

The institutional framework for carrying out the tasks at (a) and (b) above are made available from 8 Technical Committees (TCs) which provide technical advice to the supplies wing to achieve these objectives. Each committee is headed by a technical officer of the rank of Major General/ Brigadier or equivalent. These committees conduct surveys and assess capabilities for indigenisation of items identified by them with due regard to commercial viability and strategic needs.

The technical committees are equipped to generate drawings and specification for indigenous production of hitherto imported items. A Central Technical Committee (CTC) under the chairmanship of Secretary (Defence Production & Supplies) supervises the work of the technical Committees. Purchases are made on the basis of competitive quotations from firms of proven capability and capacity. All the TCs are functioning as part of DGQA.

A scheme of national award for excellence in indigenisation was introduced from the year 1993-94. The awards for the year 1996-97 were presented to seven firms on September 23, 1998.

Permanent sample rooms are maintained in the 4 metropolitan cities to help the civil sector to familiarise itself with the requirements of the armed forces. In order to help the industry and the users to recognise issues pertaining to each other, conferences are held from time to time.

ACHIEVEMENTS

The following table gives details of items ordered and their value:

Year	*No. of systems / subsystems ordered*	*Value (Rs. in crore)*
1996-97	2279	244.77
1997-98	2097	149.14
1998-99 (up to 31.12.98)	1684	97.54

INTERACTION WITH INDUSTRY

A two-tier institutional mechanism is in existence since 1985 to foster interaction between defence services and industry for optimum utilisation of capacities available in the civil sector. It consists of an apex body headed by the Secretary, Defence Production and Supplies, and three discipline-wise functional groups in which major associations of trade and industry are represented. Apart from this a meeting was held on June 18, 1998 under the chairmanship of the

Defence Minister to explore the possibility of involving the private sector in some identified areas of defence production. The Defence Ministry held interactive discussions with representatives of industry under the aegis of the Confederation of Indian Industry (CII). It was decided to establish six joint task forces between the industry and the Ministry of Defence in furtherance of the objective of expanding "Government-Industry" participation.

ORDNANCE FACTORIES

The ordnance factories organisation consists of 39 factories, some of which are the oldest industrial establishments in the country. The first ordnance factory was established in 1801 at Cossipore, near Calcutta.

By 1947, the number of factories had grown to 16. The growth of the organisation has been particularly rapid after independence. These ordnance factories play a vital role in equipping the armed forces with weapons, ammunitions, tanks, infantry combat vehicles, transport vehicles, clothing, general stores and other equipment. These factories are geographically spread all over the country.

There are ten factories each in Maharashtra and Uttar Pradesh, six factories each in Madhya Pradesh and Tamil Nadu, four factories in West Bengal and one factory each in Andhra Pradesh, Orissa and the union territory of Chandigarh. The 16 pre-Independence ordnance factories had to contend with an inadequate civil industrial infrastructure. Besides finished stores, these had to produce basic inputs and intermediate materials. The 23 post-Independence factories are linked to the developed industrial base for supply of primary intermediate inputs.

The ordnance factories have evolved into a strategic and dedicated production base for lethal and non-lethal defence stores. Investments on their infrastructure stem from national security and strategic needs.

ORGANISATION

The ordnance factories organisation is headed by the Director General of Ordnance Factories (DGOF). In 1979, an Ordnance Factory Board was established at Calcutta as per the recommendations of Rajyadhaksa Committee. The Director General of the Ordnance Factories is the Chairman of this Board. He is assisted by 9 other members each of the rank of Additional DGOF—with several charge as indicated below:

a) Ammunition and Explosives (A&E)
b) Weapons Vehicles and Equipments (WV&E)
c) Materials and Components (M&C)
d) Armoured Vehicle (AV)
e) Ordnance Equipment and Clothing (OEF)
f) Finance
g) Personnel
h) Planning and Materials Management
i) Projects and Technical Services

OBJECTIVES

The paramount objective of the organisation is to meet the requirements of the armed forces, particularly of the Army for conventional lethal and non-lethal hardware. Self-reliance and self-sufficiency are the cornerstone of defence preparedness. Adequate and timely supply of defence stores of stringent quality specification at minimal cost is the primary consideration. The exercise is carried out under constant commitment to product improvement and indigenisation.

PRODUCTION TECHNOLOGY

Capacities exist to produce a wide range of arms and ammunitions for the Infantry, Artillery and Armoured Corps of the army, for the navy and the air force.

The factories produce military transport vehicles, infantry combat vehicles, armoured vehicles, optical and opto-electronic instruments, field cables, summer and winter uniforms, tentages, parachutes, miscellaneous leather goods, floats, bridges, general stores, civil blasting explosives, and so on.

Facilities also exist for the design and manufacture of captive special purpose machine tools for production of arms and ammunition components.

Besides supply of arms, ammunition and other items to the armed forces, the needs of police and the paramilitary organisations are also catered to. Items are also produced for the railways, public sector undertakings and other Government departments.

The ordnance factories have taken up continuous upgradation of products and manufacturing technologies to meet emerging requirements of the defence forces. The futuristic approach marks the establishment of new facilities. An expert committee was constituted on July 6,1998 to enable speedy implementation of modernisation in the appropriate areas. The committee will examine:

i) The current liabilities and infrastructure available with each ordnance factory, ongoing replacement/ renewals and new projects and recommend factory-wise modification plans.

ii) Recommend casting away low technology and graduate to high technology/sophisticated technology/ state-of-the-art technology.

iii) Work out yearwise investments keeping in view the implementation schedule.

iv) Recommend plan for basic modernisation and bringing in new product profile in a phased manner in respect of factories having low technology.

GROWTH

The ordnance factories output for sales have been steadily growing over the years with a record production achievement of Rs. 3,071 crore during 1997-98 representing an increase of more than 18 per cent over the sales of Rs. 2597 crore during 1996-97. The effort has been towards progressive enhancement in the indigenous content of items of the USSR origin. In order to maintain self-sufficiency and self-reliance in defence production, the ordnance factories are continuously adopting the latest product profile to meet requirement of services.

In 1998-99, the ordnance factories are set to achieve production for sales of Rs. 3,938 crore in accordance with the projected requirements of defence and other indentors. This will represent a growth of 25 per cent over the level obtained in 1997-98 of Rs. 3,071 crore.

HIGHLIGHTS

Some of the significant achievements in ordnance factories in last few years have been as follows:

i) Thirty-eight ordnance factories have secured certification under IS-14000/ ISO 9000.

ii) Detonator plant imported from United States of America was successfully commissioned with expertise available in ordnance factories in spite of the sanctions imposed by the US government.

iii) Production of new transport vehicles of 2.5 ton and 5/7.5 Ton capacity has been established and these vehicles are being supplied to the army.

iv) New generation of armaments having a low weight to high strength ratio, *viz*., T-72, 155 mm and 30 mm systems of armaments have been productionised in the ordnance factories.

RESEARCH AND DEVELOPMENT (R&D) ACTIVITIES

In-house R&D activities towards product and process improvements are attracting great deal of attention in the ordnance factories. Techniques of solid modelling and sensitivity analysis have been adopted in meeting the design of services stores. Some of the major achievements in these fields are as follows:

i) Aluminium Alloy Light Bridge has been developed and manufactured for the first time.

ii) Cartridge Case Gauging Machine and cartridge loading machine have been manufactured in-house saving substantial foreign exchange.

iii) Special double braid ed reinforced coaxial cable has been developed successfully.

iv) Tetryl, Styphnic Acid and Nitroguanidine have been exported to other countries.

v) 0.22" porting rifle which is in great demand has been developed for the civilian market.

vi) Successfully manufactured refine cutter for use of Navy in Chukar Pilotless target aircraft.

vii) Sustainer igniter 5 B-43 and Booster Powder Igniter 4T-20 have been designed and developed successfully for the use of navy.

DIVERSIFICATION

Capacity surplus to defence requirements are utilised for production of items for the civil market and exports. This helps in reducing unit costs, increase in turnover and enhance competitiveness through market exposures.

ENERGY CONSERVATION

Energy conservation is a continuous effort. The consumption of energy per unit of production is sought to be reduced to improve utilisation, process technology upgradation and innovative techniques.

Applications of renewable sources of energy for low temperature heating in appropriate areas are adopted. Improvement is being constantly attempted to achieve a target of 5.41 per cent energy conservation of the value of production in the current year.

POLLUTION CONTROL

Pollution control is an important concern that is monitored closely and the specified level of control has been largely achieved. Programmes have been launched in the ordnance factories organisation to achieve the objectives of the national policy on environment. Effluent and emissions are held within the specified limits, periodical environmental audits are carried out and better housekeeping is enforced as recommended in their audits..

SAFETY

The corporate safety policy has been reformed during 1996 to install stringent safety standards, safety consciousness and vigilance in the ordnance factories. Accident prone and hazardous areas have merited special concern. Safety manuals and standing instructions supplement safety policies. A disaster management plan is also prepared for contingent measures and safety committees (central and shop level) have been constituted. The use of personnel protective gear and appliances is emphasised.

Accidents are investigated thoroughly and the recommendations made by the boards of inquiry and audit teams are implemented meticulously. Periodic safety audit inspections at different levels (level-I quarterly by factory's local teams, level-II half yearly by zonal teams and level-III annually by OFB team) have been introduced. Besides, the Centre for Environmental and Explosives Safety (CEES) conducts audit inspections of ammunitions and explosives group of factories. Three regional Controllerates of Safety have been set up to enhance the efficacy of safety management. These are situated at Ambajhari (Region-I for 12 factories), Kanpur (Region-II for 11 factories) and at Avadi (Region-III for six factories). The remaining ten factories in the 7.39 ammunition and explosives group are the direct concern of the Ordnance Factory Board.

AFFORESTATION

Environment and ecological balance aspects are catered to by an ongoing programme of tree plantation in the ordnance factories. During 1998-99, over one lakh trees have been planted.

PRODUCTIVE BONUS

Productivity-linked bonus (PLB) equivalent to 32 days wages based on levels achieved during 1997-98 has been paid to eligible employees, which was the same level obtained in 1996-97.

HUMAN RESOURCE DEVELOPMENT

Training and development of officers and personnel received a fresh impetus during the year. Regional Training Institutes (RTI) provides training to group 'C' and 'D' employees of the ordnance factories. A more market oriented and competitive slant has been incorporated into the curriculum. To improve technical, managerial and conceptual skills, officers are deputed to national institutes for training.

QUALITY MANAGEMENT

Manufacture of military equipment calls for stringent

specifications and performance standards under extreme ambience. Quality improvement in every sphere of activity is therefore accorded highest attention at all levels. Out of 39 Ordnance Factories, 38 have secured accredition under IS-14000/ISO-9000.

OTHER MEASURES

An apex productivity council has been set up including representatives of the board, recognised federations, and recognised associations of non-gazetted officers, supervisors and clerical employees. At the unit level, local productivity councils exist similarly constituted. The Apex Productivity Council meets twice in an year to address productivity related matters and review the functioning of the local productivity councils. The unit level productivity councils meet monthly to examine measures for improving productivity and reducing costs.

RAJBHASHA

The following measures help implement Rajbhasha (national language):

i) Regional Rajbhasha conferences are held regularly.

ii) All the codes/manuals of the OFB have been published bilingually.

iii) Organisation of Hindi workshops for officers/employees who have passed the Pragya examination.

iv) A Rajbhasha Cell has been set up at the OFB Headquarters/ordnance factories with facility for Hindi training and stenography/typewriting.

v) Provision of electronic typewriters and bilingual computers and telex at the factories and Headquarters.

vi) Publication of Hindi magazines and observance of Hindi day/week at every factory and organising Hindi competitions.

PUBLIC SECTOR UNDERTAKINGS

The value of production in 1997-98 (Rs 6235 crore) in the Defence Public Sector Undertakings (DPSUs) registered a growth of 11 per cent over that in 1996-97 (Rs 5600 crore).

All the DPSUs have earned profit in 199798. The DPSUs have endeavoured to optimise capacity utilisation, to diversify production and cater to the civil and export market. The value of production, sales and investment of the eight defence PSUs in the last two years and the estimated values for 1998-99 and the company-wise profit during 1996-97 and 1997-98 are given in the tables.

HINDUSTAN AERONAUTICS LIMITED

The Hindustan Aeronautics Ltd. was set up in 1964 with its corporate office at Bangalore. The company has 12 divisions in six states. This is the largest public sector undertaking under the Department of Defence Production and Supplies. It was originally incorporated as a private limited company and later on converted into a public limited company on July 10, 1995. It is engaged in the design, manufacture, repair and overhaul of aircraft helicopters aero-engines, avionics, instruments and accessories.

SIGNIFICANT ACHIEVEMENTS OF HAL DURING 1998-99

Significant achievements of HAL during 1998-99 are:

i) A memorandum of understanding has been signed with Boeing USA for supply of high value work packages.

ii) The company also participated in international air shows at Paris and Singapore to develop interaction with the foreign customers.

iii) All operating divisions of the company have maintained ISO 9001/9002 standard.

iv) The company has delivered the first prototype gearbox on Kaveri Engine to be fitted in Light Combat Aircraft (LCA).

v) The aircraft division of the company manufacture crashworthy panels for Advanced Light Helicopter (ALH). This could be achieved by using carved machine.

vi) The Director General of Civil Aviation has approved the Lucknow division of the company to undertake design and development of airborne parts assemblies and systems for ALH civil version.

vii) The company has paid a dividend of 20 per cent for the year 1997-98.

viii) The company was awarded "Regional Top Exporter's Shield" for the 5th consecutive year by Engineering Export Promotion Council.

BHARAT ELECTRONIC LIMITED (BEL)

The Bharat Electronics Limited, established in 1954 with its corporate office at Bangalore, has nine units in the country. It is engaged in the design, development and manufacture of sophisticated state-of-the-art electronics equipments/components for the use of defence services, paramilitary organisations and other governmental users like All India Radio, Doordarshan, Department of Telecommunications, Police Wireless, Meteorological Department and so on. The BEL is also the premier indigenous source for professional electronic equipment.

HIGHLIGHTS

Significant achievements of BEL during 1998-99 are:

i) State-of-the-art manufacturing testing and quality assurance facility has been set up in all units of BEL. Online computerisation for materials management state-of-the-art test facilities, facilities for carrying out environment and reliability checks, electromagnetic interference/electromagnetic compatibility testing facility, antenna testing facility, backup support from standardisation technical information and documentation, computer-aided design and manufacture have made BEL a modern professional electronic company.

ii) All manufacturing division/units of BEL have been accredited with ISO 9002/ISO 9001. Three divisions/units of the company-upgraded to ISO 9001.

iii) The company has entered into a joint venture with M/s GE-BE Private Ltd. for High End Rotating Anode Medical Diagnostic-X-Ray tube called CT MAX.

iv) The company won the 'Golden Peacock' National Quality Award for outstanding achievement in pursuit of Total Quality.

v) The company won the Department of Scientific and Industrial Research (DSIR) National Award, 1998, for R&D effort in industry in the area of successful commercialisation of public funded R&D.

BHARAT EARTH MOVERS LIMITED (BEML)

The Bharat Earth Movers Limited was incorporated in May 1964 and commenced operations from January 1, 1965. The production units of the company are located at Bangalore, Kolar Gold Fields (KGF) and Mysore in Karnataka.

The company is engaged in the production of rail coaches, rail bus and DC EMUs for Indian railways, heavy duty trucks/its variants, crash fire tenders, heavy recovery vehicles, PMS bridges, earth moving equipment and aggregates for defence. Its other major customers in the country are Coal India Limited, Neyveli Lignite Corporation, Associated Cement Company, the Steel Authority of India Limited, the National Hydro Electric Power Corporation and the National Thermal Power Corporation.

HIGHLIGHTS

Some salient achievements of BEML during the year are as follows:

i) The company has won export performance award for achieving highest performance in export among non-ISI members during 1996-97.

ii) National award for 1997 for being the outstanding employer of the physically handicapped.

MAZAGON DOCKS LIMITED (MDL)

Mazagon Docks Limited, established on May 13, 1960, is the premier defence shipyard in the country with a capacity to build warships up to 6,000 DWT and merchant ship up to 27,000 DWT. Its product range includes submarines, missile boats destroyers, frigates and corvettes for the Indian navy and patrol vessels for the coast guard. It has diversified products for the oil exploration sector through production and installation of wellhead platforms and diving services for coating/laying subsea pipelines.

Significant events during the year have been:

i) Medium refit and modernisation of submarine Shishumar being undertaken at East Yard of the company. This type of work is being done for the first time in India.

ii) The shipbuilding division of the company has been awarded ISO 9001 certificate for design development production installation, servicing and repairs of surface ships and floating crafts. The company declared a dividend of 20 per cent for the year 1997-98 after a gap of 13 years. This could be achieved by the dedicated efforts made by employees of the company.

iii) Repairs of INS Nashak, *INS Vipul, INS Subhadra, SSK Pontoon, CGS Vijaya* and four merchant vessels are also being undertaken.

iv) The company has manufactured and supplied B-55 Well Head Platform and 7-Clamp, on Project to Oil and Natural Gas Commission in November 1998.

v) An order for civil shipbuilding project of RSDP has been received. Besides this, one fast missile boat is also under construction.

GARDEN REACH SHIPBUILDERS & ENGINEERS LTD (GRSE)

The Garden Reach Shipbuilders and Engineers Ltd was incorporated as a joint stock company in 1934, under the name M/s Garden Reach Workshop Ltd (GRW). The Government of India acquired the company in 1960 and was re-christened it as Garden Reach Shipbuilders and Engineers Limited (GRSE).

Since then, it has grown and diversified its activities and is now a multi-unit shipyard with shipbuilding division, engineering and engine divisions. The company builds and repairs warships and auxiliary vessels for the navy and the coast guard. Its product range includes frigate carrier and oil tankers, patrol vessels, attack craft high technology, ship-borne equipment, portable bailey type steel bridges, turbine pumps for the agricultural sector, marine sewage treatment plants, diesel engines, and so on.

Its significant achievements during the year have been:

i) A Memorandum of Understanding (MOU) has been signed between GRSE and M/s Sudmash Proletarsky Zavod, Russia, for technology transfer and indigenous manufacture of stabilisers, steering gears and desalination plants at GRSE.

ii) *INS KORA* was commissioned by the Defence Minister on August 10,1998. It is the first of the series of the project P-25A.

iii) The company launched fast attack aircraft, INS DB-T-61 on September 21, 1998.

iv) The keel of the 3rd fast attack craft GRSE *Yard No. 2049* was laid on October 12,1998.

v) The chemical laboratory of GRSE was certified by the National Accreditation Board for Testing Laboratory. This is the second chemical laboratory in the country to earn this distinction.

GOA SHIPYARD LIMITED (GSL)

The Goa Shipyard Limited, established in 1957, essentially builds small and medium-size naval vessels. It is a compact, efficient and highly profitable yard.

Its significant achievements during the year have been:

i) The company has received a contract from M/s FTCEE, Netherlands, for building two special-purpose port cranes.

ii) The company has signed an MOU with M/s acb LIPS of France for collaboration in India on project-to-project basis and for manufacturing of part or full stem gear in India.

iii) A Memorandum of Understanding has been signed with Severnoye Design Bureau of Russia for the construction of rescue craft for the Indian navy.

iv) *Survey Vessel-I Yard No. 1171* was launched on April 28, 1998.

v) Extra fast attack craft-1, *Yard No. 1175* was delivered on May 14, 1998.

The Goa Shipyard has won export excellence certificate from Engineering Export Council for Promotion for highest export performance.

BHARAT DYNAMICS LIMITED (BDL)

The Bharat Dynamics Limited was set up in 1970 for manufacture of guided missiles. It is among a few strategic industries in the world and possesses the capability to produce advanced guided missile systems. The company has two units, one at Kanchanbagh and the other at Medak. Besides the indigenous Prithvi missile, it produces the French-origin Milan missile and the Russian origin Konkurs missile. It produces small arms and missiles under development by DRDO.

BDL's important achievements during the year have been:

i) Progressive indigenisation up to 70 per cent has been achieved for Milan missile. The saving of Rs. 8 lakhs per missile due to indigenisation have been passed on to the army by reducing the sale price.

ii) The company has achieved substantial progress in absorbing DRDO technology for manufacture of missiles and has been awarded in October 1997 with DRDO Technology Assimilation Award 1996.

iii) Milan and Konkur divisions have been accorded ISO 9002 accredition in 1996-97 and 1997-98, respectively.

iv) BDL has been categorised as Mini Ratna Category-I as per the Department of Public Enterprises guidelines.

MISHRA DHATU NIGAM LIMITED (MIDHANI)

MIDHANI Limited set up on November 20, 1973, manufactures special steel, titanium and super alloys required in the aeronautics, space and atomic energy engineering and communication sectors. It contributes to import substitution and self-reliance in strategic sectors.

The achievements during the year have been:

i) MIDHANI was awarded certificate of merit for consistent supply of indigenous aviation materials on September 20,1998 during the National Seminar on Indigenisation and Vendor Development.

ii) The company has been bestowed with Federation of Indian Chambers of Commerce and Industry (FICCI) Award 1997-98 for corporate initiative for research in science and technology.

iii) Advance metals and alloys for cryogenic engine application in space were developed and supplied.

iv) A new salt bath for pickling shop for the descaling of superalloy and titanium alloy materials was indigenously designed and commissioned by the company, thereby saving foreign exchange.

OTHER ORGANISATIONS OF DDP & S

Directorate General of Quality Assurance (DGQA)

The effectiveness of the armed forces depends on the reliable and consistent performance of their weapons and equipment.

The Directorate General of Quality Assurance is responsible for ensuring high precision and quality in respect of stores for the army, the navy (excluding naval armaments) and all command users items for the air force.

The DGQA is constituted into various compatible disciplines and each headed by a Technical Directorate.

The organisation discharges its functions through a chain of controllerates, quality assurance establishments and proof establishments.

The DGQA role includes:

a) Preparation of drawings and specifications.

b) Establishment of sources for procurement.

c) Testing and evaluation of samples.

d) Compilation of literature and documentation.

e) Product improvement based on the feedback.

f) The DGQA keeps close liaison and maintains interaction with the civil sector from the initial stage of development and productionisation of components and products.

The value of stores inspected and accepted during the years 1996-97, 1997-98 and 199899 are given below:

(Value in crore)

Year	Inspected	Accepted
1996-97	7106.02	6247.41
1997-98	7031.59	6367.82
1998-99 (up to 31.12.98)	5106.73	4512.72

DIRECTORATE GENERAL AERONAUTICAL QUALITY ASSURANCE (DGAQA)

The Directorate General Aeronautical Quality Assurance (DGAQA) has its headquarters at New Delhi with inspection establishment situated at various production centres. It performs the following functions:

a) Quality assurance to aeronautical specifications during design and development, inspection of equipment, quality assurance of aircraft and engine overhauled by HAL, technical assurance inspection of imported aeronautical items procured by the air force and screening indents for imports keeping in view the indigenous availability.

b) The DGAQA inspected aeronautical stores of the value of Rs. 594.83 crore up to October 1998. Aeronautical stores of the value of Rs. 600 crore inspected during the period from November 1998 to March 1999.

c) The DGAQA associated itself with indigenous aeronautics development projects from prototype to proof. It participates in defect and accident investi-gations and suggest remedial measures.

DIRECTORATE STANDARDISATION

The Directorate of Standardisation was constituted in 1962 with the objective of controlling item proliferation within the defence services. To give greater thrust to the standardisation activity, nine standardisation cells were located at nodal stations in the country under the directorate.

The primary objective of the Directorate of Standardisation is to establish commonality in equipment and components among the three services to reduce the overall inventory of the defence services. The objectives assigned, are:

a) Preparation of standardisation documents for the joint services such as specifications, preferred ranges, rationalised lists, guides, policy statements and qualitative requirements.
b) Eighty-four catalogues covering main equipment/ assemblies, sub-assemblies have been published till October 1998. Approximately 3,48,595 items have been codified so far which is 82.71 per cent of the target for current year, and 72,642 items are expected to be completed by the end of this year.

DIRECTORATE OF PLANNING AND COORDINATION

The Directorate of Planning and Coordination was set up in 1964 with the primary objective of preparing overall plans for the production of defence equipment in the country. In furtherance of its role, the directorate represents the Department of Defence Production and Supplies in General Staff Equipment Policy, the R&D panels, standardisation committees, task forces and various monitoring committees. The directorate also represents the Department of Defence Production & Supplies (DDP&S) in the licensing committee meetings of the Ministry of Industry to ensure that there is no overlap in the capacities created elsewhere and under the Ministry of Defence. The directorate is also responsible for processing the cases of setting up of ordnance factories in the country at the green field site and monitor implementation of major projects relating to ordnance factories. In addition, it coordinates matters relating to indigenisation of defence hardware and monitoring of budget of the Ordnance Factory Board. The directorate is the nodal point in the department for international cooperation on defence production and defence exports.

Besides indigenous manufacture of armoured vehicles, setting up of facilities for manufacture and filling of high calibre ammunition as well as for overhaul of tanks and their engines, manufacture of sights and laser range finder for defence, product improvement of artillery guns and limited series production of Main Battle Tank *Arjun* are some of the major programmes currently being progressed by the directorate.

DEFENCE EXHIBITION ORGANISATION

The Defence Exhibition Organisation (DEO), established in 1981, is primarily responsible for organising and coordinating defence exhibitions in India and abroad. It maintains permanent defence exhibition pavilions at Pragati Maidan, New Delhi. The Ordnance Factory Board, Defence Public Sector Undertakings (DPSUs), Defence Research and Development Organisation (DRDO), Directorate General of Quality Assurance (DGQA), the three services, the Coast Guard and the National Cadet Corps (NCC) are represented in the exhibition. Products manufactured by the ordnance factories and the defence public sector undertakings are displayed in the pavilion to provide an overview of the wide range of defence infrastructure in the country.

The defence exhibition organisation participated in the India International Trade Fair and won a Gold Medal for excellence in display during IITF 98. The organisation played an important role in conducting the Aero India 98 by the Department of Defence Production and Supplies during December 8-12, 1998. The major Indian participants included defence production units, DRDO, ISRO, International Airport Authority of India and companies in the private sector engaged in the manufacture of components, spare parts, and so on for the aeronautical/ aerospace industries. There was major participation from abroad, which includes representation from the United Kingdom, Russia, France, Israel, and so on. Over 110 companies from 17 foreign countries and 62 companies from India, which included almost all renowned names in the aeronautics/ aerospace industry participated in the event. At the invitation of the Ministry of Defence, 15 foreign defence delegations visited Aero India 98.

9

Defence Research and Development

The Department of Defence Research and Development is dedicatedly working towards enhancing self-reliance in defence systems. The department undertakes design and development leading to production of world-class weapon systems and equipment in accordance with the expressed needs and the qualitative requirements laid down by the three services.

Research and Development (R&D) Programmes

The department undertakes staff projects/ programmes for development of defence systems and R&D programmes in areas of emerging and futuristic technologies to build up expertise, competence and competitive edge. In order to minimise the vulnerability to various technology control regimes instituted by the advanced countries, thrust is given to development of critical components, technologies and infrastructure.

Programme Management and Review Structure

The department executes various research and development programmes/projects through a network of 51 laboratories/ establishments. The Aeronautical Development Agency (ADA), a society funded by the department, is engaged in the development of Light Combat Aircraft (LCA). The department has adopted the development strategy of consortia partnership with academic institutions, R&D laboratories of other departments and industry in the public and the private sector for making optimum use of science and technology (S&T) expertise, technical knowhow and industrial infrastructure available in the country. Complex technological programmes are managed by multi-tier management boards which ensure multi-layered reviews and monitoring facilitating quick coordination, problem-solving and smooth execution of the programmes /projects.

Depending upon the cost and technical complexity of programmes, review processes have been instituted which include both in-house and external panels, steering committees, peer group and so on. The programmes are also reviewed at the apex level by the DRDO Council, chaired by SA to RM and at the levels of Service Chiefs and the Defence Minister.

These reviews are carried-out with active participation of representatives of the user services, production agencies and quality assurance organisations. In order to shorten the time cycle between completion of development and productionisation of defence systems, techniques of 'Concurrent Engineering' and 'Real Time Technology Absorption' are being used in some cases of the complex programmes/ projects.

PROGRESS MADE IN 1998-1999

Progress made in the integrated Guided Missile Development Programme, which envisages development, leading to production, of four missiles, namely *Prithvi*, *Trisul*, *Akash* and *Nag* and a re-entry technology demonstration project *Agni*, is given below:

The government have approved the development of a longer range version of *Agni* based on the state-of-the-art technologies developed indigenously.

Surface-to-surface missile *Prithvi P-II* (air force version) is getting ready for user trials. Flight trials are scheduled during February 1999. Static tests of pre-fragmented variable mass warhead for *Prithvi* were carried out during October 1998. The launcher stabilisation system for the naval version of *Prithvi* has been designed, fabricated, installed and is under testing.

Two flight trials of quick reaction short range surface-to-air missile *Trisul* for Army (one against moving line of sight and another against moving target) were conducted. Five flight trials of the naval version of *Trisul* were conducted from *INS Dronacharya* against simulated target and in anti-sea skimmer role achieving all the mission objectives. Missile Command Post (MCP) trials were conducted to establish communication and interface software using fly-catcher radar and MCP. Four flight trials of third generation tank missile *Nag* were carried out successfully during July-August 1998 in which two were ballistic flights and two were control flights with tube launch.

Five tests of tandem warhead in flight configuration have been carried out. Type-certified twin launchers with dummy missiles have been realised and placed at Helicopter Design Bureau of the Hindustan Aeronautics Limited for facilitating *Alhnag* system integration. Three flight trials of medium range surface-to-air missile *Akash* were conducted successfully during August and September, 1998. Two flights were undertaken against simulated targets and one flight was undertaken against a moving target *Nishant*.

The phased array radar, *Rajendra* in weapon control mode has been successfully proved in these guided flight trials. Another unit of battery level radar (BLR) and battery control centre (BCC) is under process of realisation. Development of 3-dimensional central acquisition radar (CAR) was under prgress. The phase-I of the engine ground run of the first technology demonstrator (TD-I) LCA has been completed. The aircraft is under preparation for low-speed taxi trials planned for the first quarter of 1999.

The second LCA technology demonstrator (TD-2) was rolled out in August 1998 and its system integration has commenced. The impact of US sanctions on LCA programme has been analysed. These sanctions have caused a delay of six months in the maiden flight of LCA, which was now scheduled to take place by mid-1999. A national team of experts constituted to develop flight control system (FCS) using alternate sources has successfully developed the software for FCS.

The project definition phase of the naval version LCA has been completed. Five prototype vehicles PV1 to PV5 are planned apart from two technology demonstrators so as to accelerate the process of testing and type certification, thereby reducing the development timeframe. These prototype vehicles are at various stages of fabrication and assembly. A virtual reality centre for creating and studying of LCA virtual prototype has been established at ADA.

Five prototypes of *Kaveri* engine have undergone extensive ground testing for a period of 369 hours and a total of about 900 hours have been logged so far. All the development trials of indigenously developed *Kaveri* Engine Digital Electronic Control System (KADECS) have been carried out. The efficacy of the digital control system has been established. The design of weight budgeted flight standard engine has been completed and the manufacture of ten engine prototypes has been launched to meet the programme requirement.

Altitude testing on *Kabini* the core engine of *Kaveri* has been successfully completed at high altitude facility at Central Institute of Aviation Motors (CIAM), Moscow. The demonstration of successful functioning of afterburner in the *Kaveri* engine has been carried out. There has been a major thrust for the indigenisation of materials for the programme and 90 per cent of indigenously developed super alloy materials have been certified.

A joint team drawn from different organisations including Air Force, has completed the review on all aspects of integration of *Kaveri* engine on the Flying Test Bed at Moscow. The design phase study of *Kaveri* marinisation project has been successfully completed. Twelve flight trials of *Nishant* carried out during the year have successfully demonstrated the reliable launch and damage free recovery operation, accurate way-point navigation capabilities, ability to fly pre-programmed or manually controlled trajectories, capability of being used as aerial target for surface to air missile evaluation, satisfactory operation of gim-balled payload assembly, video tracker and daylight TV camera system.

The design and development of Aerostat, a payload-carrying tethered balloon, has been underaken. Experimental trials of balloon imaging and surveillance system (BLISS) have been carried out. Two aerostats, having 95 and 160 cubic metre capacities respectively, were successfully deployed carrying LLTV camera for optical reconnaissance. Dropping system to drop heavy loads upto 3000 kg from AN-32 aircraft using a cluster of parachutes has been developed. The system has been proved successful in technical trials. The INSAS rifle (fixed butt) of 5. 56 mm calibre and LMG are under bulk production and a common large quantity of these, along with ammunition for the INSAS family of small arms, has been issued to the army. The folding butt version of 5.56 mm INSAS rifle has also been accepted for introduction into service.

The Multi-Barrel Rocket System *Pinaka* has been further refined and its accuracy, consistency, safety and reliability aspects have been successfully demonstrated to the users. Extended user trials of the system were planned for early 1999. The user trials of DRDO developed emission type smoke bomb for 120 mm mortar have been successfully completed and the ammunition has been accepted for introduction into service.

Heavy destruction charges capable of neutralising unexploded bombs embedded into the ground were successfully subjected to user application trials and have been accepted for introduction into service. The indigenously developed ammunition for Automatic Grenade Launcher (Ex Russia) AGS-17, after acceptance by the army, has entered the production phase.

The 15 pre-production series (PPS) main battle tank (MBT) *Arjun* tanks delivered by DRDO to the Army have been subjected to exhaustive automotive and weapon system trials during 1998. The trials have clearly established the efficacy of *MBT Arjun* weapon system even in the worst adverse weather conditions. A Joint Action Plan (JAP) has been jointly formulated by the users and DRDO. The modifications identified in JAP have been implemented for series production.

The government has accorded clearance for production of *MBT Arjun* to equip two regiments of army. The army has placed an indent for bulk manufacture of Carrier Mortar Tracked (CMT) on the production agency—Ordnance Factory, Medak. All the production drawings and technology for manufacture of CMT have been handed over by DRDO to the production agency. BHIM T-6 self-propelled (SP) gun comprising of 155 mm 52 calibre, mounted on T-6 Turret of *LIW South Africa*, on the *MBT Arjun* derivative chassis has been integrated. The user evaluation trials of this gun were conducted during July-August 1998.

Certain snags in the T-6 turret system have been observed. The retrials of the BHIM T-6 SP gun with improved and ruggedised turret were conducted during April-June 1999. The smoke grenades currently in service can obscure the tanks from laser beams only with the advent of thermal imaging sight and a need was felt to develop a smoke composition which can obscure tank for thermal sight also.

The trials of the indigenously developed anti laser and anti-thermal Smoke Grenades (SMGD) were conducted from T-72 M1 Tank by the army 8.31 during day and night in October 1998. The efficacy of these smoke grenades has been proved successfully during these trials. One T-72 engine has been successfully uprated from 780 HP to 1000 HP. Limited automotive trials of the T-72 M1 tank integrated with uprated 1000 HP T-72 engine were conducted during 1998. Two T-72 M1 tanks, integrated with uprated 1000 HP engines, were offered to users for trials during summer 1999.

All automotive trials of Armoured Engineer Reconnaissance Vehicle (AERV) which provides a capability to acquire, record and transmit data on width, bed profile, water depth and bearing capacity of the surface of remote and inaccessible areas have been successfully completed. A multi-axled extra long transporter in 12×8 configuration has been developed for transportation and deployment of heavy military hardware like bridges and missiles and so on. The payload capacity of the vehicle is 23 tonne and it can carry systems having a length up to 23 metre.

The composite sonar system and tactical weapon control system (*Panchendriya*) comprising active and passive sonars have been developed and installed on board a submarine for users' trials. After successful completion of harbour acceptance trials (HATs), *Panchendriya* has been accepted in sea acceptance tests (SATs) also. The upgraded version of Hull Mounted Sonar (HUMSA) has completed 168 hours of factory acceptance tests (FATs). The system will be fitted on board ship under construction at Garden Reach Shipbuilders and Engineers (GRSE), Calcutta. After completion of its integration, the airborne sonar system, MIHIR, with capabilities for processing data from sonobuoy, has been completed. The system has been fitted on board an aircraft and high speed trials have been successfully completed.

Technical trials of Advanced Experimental Torpedo (AET) were completed in October 1998. The production agency, Bharat Dynamics Limited (BDL), has been actively associated in trials to facilitate quick transfer of technology. Forty dynamic trials of Wire Guided Torpedo (WGT) have been conducted. Vehicle dynamics, propulsion system, control system, on-board computer and recovery aids have been proven. Further trials are in progress and are expected to be completed by June 1999. User trials of Processor-based Moored Mine (PBMM) for magnetic, acoustic and pressure influences of ships are in progress since June 1998 and were expected to be completed by June 1999.

Fuel cell of 1Kw capacity has been successfully developed. Utilising this technology, development of high capacity power pack has been taken up for defence applications. All entities required for the Core System Demonstration (CSD) of the communication segment of integrated electronic warfare system *Samyukta* have been realised, integrated and tested along with their embedded software. Systems software is now being tested after which the communication segment will be offered for demonstration.

Laboratory models of two entities of *Sangraha* programme intended for naval helicopters and light aircraft, have been demonstrated to the users and the engineered versions are being fabricated for field evaluation. The third entity is getting ready for demonstration by March 1999. The development of TEMPEST EW system for the air force has been completed. The Gallium Arsenide Enabling Technology Centre (GAETEC) has commenced production of monolithic microwave integrated circuits (MMICs) using DRDO developed technology.

The MMIC amplifier modules fabricated at the centre have been evaluated by user laboratories and quality assurance agency and are recommended for trials in the existing air defence system. The centre has taken up to supply MMIC modules to the department of space also. MMIC switch technology has also been developed and transferred to GAETEC. Satcom terminals in S-band have been developed and communications established using the S-band transponder provided on INSAT series of satellites.

A self-contained digester for disposal of human waste by microbial degradation in an eoo-friendly manner for high altitude has been developed. The digesters installed at various high altitude areas are functioning satisfactorily with no foul smell. Solution gel technologies for silicon-dioxide base composites for applications in radomes has been developed. Speciality materials such as semarium, cobalt, tungsten, nickel, cobalt and alumina ceramic sintered tubes for gyro components have been successfully developed.

A technique for adoption of existing fluoroscopic machines for Computed Tomography (CT) imaging to visualise crosssection details of various components has been developed. Tissue bank facility has been created for preparation of radiation processed chorioamnion grafts. The grafts are extremely useful for treating burn injuries. The facility can provide 2,000 grafts per year. A new concept of building for storage of propellants based on unit risk principle, which restricts the loss of valuable stocks to the affected location only, has been validated by field trials. The design provides considerable saving in real estate requirement with much improved safety. Likewise design of magazine for storage of mass detonating explosives has been established by technical trials.

With this design, saving of land up to 75 per cent has been made feasible. The DRDO has carried out comprehensive fire safety reviews periodically for augmenting fire safety in various establishments under the Ministry of Defence. Necessary guidelines on fire protection and preventive measures have been issued to these establishments. Carbon nano tubes which have potential application in pharmaceuticals, electronics, high-tech composites, strategic and smart materials, have been produced in small quantities.

Fibre Reinforced Plastic (FRP) composite with conducting fabric on both sides has been developed for the fabrication of composite cabinet for housing high power radar transmitter on aircraft. The composite material gives a shielding effect in desired frequency range. Trials of armoured amphibious dozer were completed during the year and it is now under final evaluation for acceptance. Mechanically launched trestle-cum-span bridging system *Sarvatra* which can overcome obstacles up to 70 metre length, extendable to 100 metres, suitable for heaviest tracked vehicles is undergoing the final phase of trials.

Mountaineering equipment developed by DRDO were successfully used by Tata Everest India 1998 expedition, which hoisted the tricolour atop Mount Everest on May 19, 1998. The range of mountaineering equipment developed by DRDO include ice hammer, ice pitons, rock pitons, piton hammer, crampons, ice wall climbing and crevasse crossing ladders and evacuation sledges and so on.

State-of-the-art Automatic Weather Stations (AWS), for gathering a real time snow, avalanche and meteorological data developed in 1997-98 have undergone extensive field trial in hostile environmental conditions of J&K. Avalanche warnings with accuracy of 65-80 per cent were issued for areas of J&K including Siachen and Himachal Pradesh. Five such AWS were installed in the glacial environment on Siachen & J&K areas at altitudes of about 4,000 metres. Seven more AWS are under installation at other places in the remote areas of J&K.

These stations are collecting real time data through highly rugged sensors round the clock and transmitting the same to an earth receiving station installed at SASE Research & Development Centre, Ramgarh. Two such systems are also being installed in Antarctica during the year. Installation and commissioning of AWS in remote places have opened a new era for accessing snow, avalanche and meteorological conditions of inaccessible areas on real time basis for issuing of advance warning to the civil and army population from unforeseen natural disasters like avalanches, landslides, slush-flow and so on.

Remote sensing of snow cover and avalanche parameters has been undertaken by DRDO to detect pressure of various types of moraine and crevasses in the glacier region. Avalanche control through structures in formation zone has been taken up on systematic lines as a new programme under a project.

Structures like snow fences, jet roofs have been erected in the higher reaches of Jammu-Srinagar National Highway for preventing cornice formation and snow accumulation in the avalanche-formation zone. Installation of a mechanical device known as *Sprengbahn* for carriage of explosives to the desired place in formation zone for artificial triggering of avalanches is in progress. DRDO also provides engineering support to the national programme of Antarctica expedition. A scientist of DRDO was selected as a station commander of Maitri Station for the XVII Indian Antarctic Expedition. The fuel-cell technology was installed for the first time in the icy continent of Antarctica, demonstrating clean and pollution free environment of power source possibility at Maitri station.

SUPPORT TO SERVICE

Efforts of DRDO for growing vegetables and imparting training to local farmers in extreme cold deserts/high altitude regions have resulted in augmenting the production and supply of fresh vegetables to the troops deployed in the cold desert/high altitude regions. DRDO has undertaken plans to expand its operations at Partapur in the Nubra Valley of Ladakh region for demonstration of mass-scale vegetable production including greenhouse cultivation in winters and breeding of livestock and poultry.

An experimental dairy has been started at Partapur resulting in production and supply of approximately 200 litres of milk per day to the troops in Siachen. The DRDO has developed Meals-Ready-to-Eat (MRE) ration packs for marine divers and commandos. The prototype of this ration have been supplied to *INS Abhimanyu* and *INS Kalinga* for user acceptance trials. The ration has a shelf-life of one year. The users have appreciated the MIZE and out li importance in various operations. Malaria detection/ control camps were organised with the help of the Mobile Malaria Clinic developed by the DRDO in various Army cantonments and villages as well as in the north-east region.

The DRDO has been assisting the services in training of jawans in agro-technologies thus helping them in their rehabilitation. The DRDO developed a much efficient and effective two phase selection system to reduce unwanted and unduly heavy workload on recruitment and selection boards for the armed forces. The newly developed system screens out 40-50 per cent of candidates who *prima-facie* do not possess the required attributes in the significant measures.

The system was approved by the government in October 1998. Apart from reducing the effort from assessors the new system has also improved the quality of manpower intake and reduce the time and cost involved in the process. The DRDO is also providing assistance to the services in life evaluation of various type of missiles held in their inventory.

HUMAN RESOURCE DEVELOPMENT

The DRDO has been giving a major thrust in motivating the human resource engaged in the research and development activities. The organisation has been conscious about its personnel policies to provide desired career advancements for all categories of personnel. The successful operation of Defence Research and Development Services (DRDS) for its Scientists and Defence Research and Technical Cadre (DRTC) for technical cadres speak of these progressive policies adopted by the DRDO. After the implementation of the V Central Pay Commission a massive exercise of cadre review for its Group 'C' and 'D' (non-technical) staff was undertaken for providing them adequate career advancement.

As a result of this exercise, the stagnation level in most of the Group 'C' categories has been brought down from 15

22 years to 8-12 years. Consequent upon the cadre review, nearly 1,500 Group 'C' and 1,275 Group 'D' employees of the organisation have been benefited. Due to the fast changing environment on account of liberalisation and globalisation, there has been an unprecedented higher rate of attrition of the scientists/engineers in the field of electronics and computer engineering for the last few years. Efforts have been made to fill up the deficiencies through campus recruitments and open advertisements. The government has approved of a package of incentives to the scientists to make the DRDS attractive.

CO-OPERATION WITH UNIVERSITIES & ACADEMIC INSTITUTIONS

The DRDO sponsors M.E./M.Tech/M.Sc. courses, in order to keep pace with new research and technologies at the university level and other academic institutions. Forty personnel of the DRDO were sponsored for such courses in 28 different disciplines covering 11 universities/institutions. To undertake research in newer frontiers of technology, three more research boards, namely, the Life Sciences Research Board, the Naval Research Board and the Armament Research Board have been formed apart from the already existing Aeronautical Research and Development Board.

Four officers joined the MBA programme at Bharathi Dasan Institute of Management, Tiruchirapalli for the session 1998-2000. Continuing education programmes (CEP) are given high priority for refreshing the working knowledge of middle level managers and specialist in administration, stores and finance management. One hundred and sixty-one CEP courses were conducted for 3,420 such specialists.

In order to support consortia research with universities and academic institutions, the DRDO had supported 29 ongoing research projects to 13 institutions at a cost of 4.75 crore under the Research and training electronics scheme. There are 27 other ongoing research projects with 24 institutions involving funds of Rs 2.80 crore. The DRDO also supports research projects under MOUs with six institutions.

During the period, a total of 278 scientists/engineers were deputed abroad for technical inspection, transfer of technology, training and attending international meetings, conferences and seminars.

ISO-9000 CERTIFICATION OF DROD LABORATORIES

To upgrade the quality aspects of indigenously developed products systems, DRDO has undertaken ISO-9000 and the national accreditation board, for testing and callibration of Laboratories (NABL) certification of its laboratories. The research and development establishment (Engineers), Pune, was awarded ISO-9001 certification during 1998 for research, design, test and evaluation of combat engineering, ground systems and cold region engineering equipment for military and civil application.

INTELLECTUAL PROPERTY RIGHTS

Efforts were continued to promote awareness amongst scientists regarding safeguarding intellectual property rights (IPR) on the DRDO developed products, processes, designs and software packages. A number of presentations/ interactive meetings/short-term-courses were organised at various laboratories/establishments of the DRDO.

Scientists in the DRDO are being encouraged to file an increasing number of IPR applications and are being provided necessary techno-legal and financial support in preparation and filing of patent documents.

GOLDEN JUBILEE CELEBRATIONS OF INDEPENDANCE

The DRDO celebrated the golden jubilee on the 50th year of India's Independence by organising laboratory/ establishment level workshops, seminars, lectures and exhibitions for popularising spinoff technologies beneficial to the society. The notable activities under this programme include organising Ladakhi Kissan Mela, greening the unutilised area in laboratories/ establishments, workshops on future technology, anti-pollution drive, literacy drive, blood donation camps, release of defence technology books on different disciplines, network of desalination plants under water mission, para-sailing adventure camps and exhibitions on rails.

The programme was concluded by the DRDO participation in exhibition on 'India's Vision for the Future' on Rajpath lawns on August 15, 1998 in which alive display of *Prithvi* on a mobile launcher, *MBT, INDRA* Radar, RPV *Nishant* and balloon barrage system was organised.

SOCIETAL MISSION AS SPINOFF DEFENCE TECHNIQUES

Artificial lower limb both below and above the knee having a modular design with light weight composite material has been developed. The technology used in this development has been world class and weight of the limb is only 1.2 g. The limb is providing near normal gait for the user and cost of the this limb will be 20 to 25 per cent less than that of a similar imported version. The limb is undergoing user/ technical trials at Artificial Limb Centre, Pune, and at Mobility India, Bangalore. The NBC respirator mask, leak tester, resuscitator, hood mask and hapo bag Mk II are already in production. Functional Electrical Simulators (FES) for paraplegics, and the ventilator for comatose patients are undergoing type-certification.

10

Inter-Service Organisations

Military Engineer Services (MES)

The largest construction agency of the country, the Military Engineer Services (MES), provides works cover in 450 stations spread across the country in peace areas as well as in forward areas. It is the premier engineering arm of the Ministry of Defence which provides works services to the three defence services and other related departments, such as the Defence Research and Development Organisation, Directorate General of Quality Assurance, Ordnance Factories, Coast Guard, Kendriya Vidyalaya Sangathan, Central and state government undertakings.

The MES has a long and eventful history and has come of age, growing along with the engineering profession and the needs of the modern hi-tech armed forces of independent India. Today, it handles an annual workload which exceeds Rs. 2,300 crore. MES functions under the overall control of the Engineer-in-Chief, who is the adviser to the Ministry of Defence and the three services on construction engineering.

It is structured to design works which are executed through contracts under the supervision of officers and staff consisting of both civilians and combatants from the Corps of Engineers. It has an integral multidisciplinary team of architects, civil, electrical and mechanical engineers, structural designers, quantity surveyors and contract specialists for planning, designing and supervision of works. While the officers cadre has an All India Service liability, the subordinates are restricted to area-based requirements. MES has specialised in a wide spectrum of civil works, ranging from conventional buildings and factories to sophisticated complex laboratories, marine works, jetties, dockyards, wharves, workshops, slipways, air fields, roads, blast pens, and so on.

It also provides sophisticated infrastructural services like air-conditioning, cold storage, water supply, compressed air, sewage-treatment plants, lifts, cranes, and so on for the defence services. A few important timebound projects completed/in progress by the MES during 1997-98 and 1998-99 are given below:

COMPLETED WORKS

i) *Provision of Other Than Married (OTM) Accommodation at Jodhpur for 76 Medium Regiment at Jodhpur*: Work was sanctioned by the Government of India in May 1996 at an estimated cost of Rs. 543 lakhs. The work was completed in September 1997 well before the probable date of commencement.

ii) *Project Quick Shelter (Phase-I)*: Quick shelter project at a cost of Rs. 164.13 crore covering 42 high pressure stations of 6,966 dwelling units was sanctioned by the government in 1995-96. Out of this, works at 39 stations consisting of 6,894 dwelling units have been completed and put into use.

iii) *Single Officers Accommodation for 164 Officers at Mhow:* This project was sanctioned on November 29, 1994, and was completed on June 28, 1998. The total cost of the project is Rs. 633 lakhs. The buildings are in the process of being handed over to the users.

iv) *Para II Work—Provision of Accommodation for 2x Air Operational Flights and Base facilities for Army Aviation Base at Jodhpur*: An important work for provision of Accommodation for two air operation flights and base facilities for army aviation base at Jodhpur costing Rs. 1,132.48 lakhs was sanctioned under Para 11. This work has been completed within the scheduled date of completion *i.e.*, June 30, 1998.

v) *Introduction of pre-fabricated construction of married accommodation at Gurgaon*: A pilot project for construction of 168 married quarters for sergeants in air force has been taken up at an estimated cost of Rs. 5.27 crore. The building elements comprised auto-claved aerated precast concrete slabs manufactured under controlled condition in a factory. This type of construction has some major advantages like superior and uniform quality, faster mode of construction, environment friendly, better thermal and sound insulation and low-maintenance cost. The buildings have been completed in little more than one year, much earlier than the scheduled date of completion and are in the process of being occupied.

vi) *International Aero-Space Exhibition-98 at Yelahanka*: The infrastructure work costing approx. Rs. 10 crore was entrusted to MES. It involved augmenting covered display space for the exhibition by constructing a new hanger with annexes, improving manoeuvering facility by providing additional hand standings, dispersals and utility building for exhibitors maintenance personnel. The work was required to be completed in a strict time schedule of 10 months, which has been completed in time. Similar task was entrusted in 1996 also. On both the occasions, MES has displayed a commendable capability to provide the infrastructure within the time schedule and of high quality.

vii) *Under water ranges at Goa:* The project comprises a offshore and onshore works costing Rs. 1.54 crore and Rs. 1.68 crore respectively. The technical and administrative complex of the project was completed on June 30, 1998. A high standard of work achieved by Chief Engineer (navy) has been commended by the Chairman, Technical Standing Committee of this project.

viii) *Repair facilities for torpedos at Naval Advance Depot (NAD), Trombay*: The work, comprising a workshop (fully air-conditioned) and a service block, was constructed at a cost of Rs. 2.31 crore and completed in October 1997.

(ix) *Controller of Defence Accounts (Navy), Mumbai*: A new seven-storey building to accommodate the office of CDA (Navy) has been constructed at a cost of Rs. 2.36 crore, adjacent to the existing Heritage Building and completed in September 1997 and has been commended by the Defence Accounts Department.

x) *Augmentation of accommodation for Naval Hospital, Powai*: The existing 20 bedded naval hospital was provided with an additional accommodation of 20 beds at a cost of Rs. 2.76 crore. The building was inaugurated by Rear Admiral P. Jaitley, VSM, Admiral Superintendent Dockyard, Mumbai on December 19,1997.

WORKS UNDER EXECUTION/PLANNING

i) *Project quick shelter (Phase II)*: During 1997-98, the government approved the Quick Shelter Project Phase 11 costing Rs. 32.1 crore covering 8 high-pressure stations of 1,119 dwelling units. The contracts for 3 stations have been accepted and the works are in progress.

ii) *Storage accommodation at Banar-Jodhpur:* A time-bound project costing Rs. 12.97 crore for storage facilities at Banar-Jodhpur is in progress.

iii) *Provision of OTM accommodation for Artillery Regiment at Kamptee*: Go ahead sanction for a prestigious work costing Rs. 26.25 crore was accorded by the government on September 7, 1998. The work shall be sanctioned under fast track procedure. The scheduled date of completion of the project is March 2001.

iv) *Provision of storage accommodation at Pulgaon*: Go ahead sanction for the prestigious work costing Rs. 25-70 crore has been accorded by Government on September 07, 1998. The work will be executed under fast-track procedure and the project is scheduled to be completed by September 2001.

v) *Provision of OTM accommodation for college of Defence Management (CDM) at Secunderabad*: A prestigious project for provision of OTM Accommodation for College of Defence Management at Secunderabad costing Rs. 613.57 lakhs was sanctioned by Government of India on March 10, 1998. The project is scheduled for completion by September 2001.

vi) *Water supply scheme at Mathura*: The project costing Rs. 891 lakhs was released on July 16, 1992 and its construction commenced on October 30, 1993. There were some hitches to ensure adequate quality of water which were overcome, though at the cost of some delay, 93 per cent of the project was completed as on September 1998.

vii) *OTM accommodation for Central Vehicle Depot (CVD) at Panagarh*: OTM accommodation for CVD at the Panagarh project costing Rs. 800.54 lakhs due to be completed on May 31, 1999. The project is being executed as per schedule and 93 per cent progress had been achieved till September, 1998 which commenced on October 27,1995.

viii) *OTM accommodation for corps HQ and 5 tactical Air Centre*: Documents for the project have been finalised and case is under process for administrative approval. The cost of the project is Rs. 641.89 lakhs. The construction is likely to be completed in 24 months.

ix) *Modernisation of Hospital for INHS Asvini Mumbai*: A prestigious Rs. 100 crore project for INHS *Asvini* (825-bedded hospital) has been taken up at Mumbai. The sanction was accorded by the government for Rs. 63.86 crore (Phase I) on December 23, 1997 and 8.71 crore (Phase II) on September 17,1998. The project involves incorporation of latest medical facilities into the existing hospital whose origin dates back to the year 1756. The new facilities have been designed to conform to the existing architecture and make optimum use of the present complex. The project is planned to be completed by the end of year 2001.

x) *Naval officers' mess at Rao Tula Ram Marg, New Delhi*: A single officers accommodation and a prestigious building for officers at Rao Tula Ram Marg, New Delhi is under progress at a cost of Rs. 805-54 lakhs. The project comprises of a main mess building including all external services. Allied facilities such as swimming pool, recreation grounds, squash courts/tennis courts of international standards have also been included in this project. The project is scheduled to be completed by mid-2000.

(xi) *Air force officer's mess, New Delhi*: This project has been sanctioned at an estimated cost of Rs.1,007.43 lakhs.

(xii) *Military hospital at Chennai*: A prestigious project for provision of 249-bedded hospital at Chennai costing

Rs. 14.92 crore was sanctioned by the government on September 2, 1997. The planning and contract action is in progress. The probable date of completion is September 2001.

(xiii) *434-bedded hospital at Jabalpur:* The project has been sanctioned by the government at an estimated cost of Rs.355 lakhs. Tenders for this project were received on February 21, 1997 and financial concurrence accorded by the government for an amount of Rs. 615 lakhs. The tender has been accepted and work is in progress. The work is likely to be completed by December 2000.

The following have been the thrust areas during the year:

Quality management: Total quality management has been the buzzword for MES. To improve the quality of works and services being provided by MES, the department has launched a drive to obtain ISO-9001 certification for the prestigious projects. Action is in hand to obtain ISO-9001 certification for the premier Design and Consultancy Establishment of Chief Engineer (Design & Consultency), Pune.

ii) *Streamlining works procedure for speedy implementation of defence projects*: In order to expedite sanctioning, planning and execution of MES works of high value, especially, the married accommodation projects, a modified procedure in the form of *Fast-track procedure* is being implemented vigorously, so as to improve the satisfaction level of troops.

iii) *Users interaction and satisfaction*: Efforts are being made to secure greater involvement of users in planning and execution of projects. The formation of Project Management Groups consisting of users, engineer executives and staff authorities is being given importance for quick decision-making on functional and technical requirements in the implementation of projects to reduce cost and time overruns. Progress achieved in this direction is satisfactory.

ARMED FORCES MEDICAL SERVICES

Mission: Ensuring sound health and medical fitness of the armed forces personnel is a critical component, for in the absence of this, these personnel would not be able to do full justice to the diverse jobs expected to be performed by them in heterogeneous environments, both on borders and while on internal security duties and this is a mission, which, the Armed Forces Medical Service (AFMS) headed by a director general is accomplishing exceedingly well. The AFMS is primarily responsible for providing comprehensive armed forces health care to the serving their families and dependants.

In personnel/and their families addition, ex-servicemen are also entitled to free treatment from services sources and so are the paramilitary organisations like the Assam Rifles, Rashtriya Rifles, Coast Guard as well as the DRDO and Border Road personnel, while posted in the non-family stations. In addition to this, life-saving emergent care is also provided to all civilians by establishments of AFMS.

Brief details of their activities are as under:

World Health Organisation (WHO) Day: This day is observed on April every year to coincide with the day of formation of WHO. To commemorate the day, WHO every year selects a subject of public health importance and give a slogan to highlight the theme. In 1998, the theme selected was 'Safe Motherhood' and the slogan was 'Pregnancy is Special—Let us make it safe. WHO Day was celebrated at all cantonments/ stations in the armed forces. An essay writing competition for women employees posted at medical, dental and nursing directorate was organised in the office of the Directorate General Armed Forces Medical Services (DGAFMS).

A health exhibition on the 'theme' was also held during the celebration. Conducting orientation courses to medical, paramedical and to paediatric and obstertric departments staff are given a certificate from UNICEF and a plaque from the National Task Force. Directions have been issued to service hospitals to adopt Baby Friendly Hospital Initiative (BFHI) and to get certificate from the UNICEF and a plaque from the National Task Force.

Central Tuberculosis Strategy for Armed Forces: Pulmonary Tuberculosis (PTB) has remained a constant challenge to the health professionals, both in the civil setting as well as in the armed forces. Inspite of improvements in various health indicators of the country, there has been no let up in the incidence of this disease. Though the treatment programme for PTB remained excellent in the armed forces, its documentation was required to be improved. Action has been initiated during the year 1998 for creation of Central Registry for Tuberculosis (CRT) for improving the documentation of PTB cases in the armed forces.

Baby Friendly Hospital Initiative (BFHI) in Service Hospitals: To ensure protection and promotion of breast-feeding, UNICEF, since 1992, have started the movement called 'The Baby Friendly Hospital initiative (BFHI)'. In India, the movement was launched in 1993. *Hospital Adopting the Policy and Medical Care of ex-Servicemen*: Medical facilities for ex-Servicemen and their families have been improved at NOIDA, Faridabad, Gurgaon and Delhi.

Super Speciality Veterans Hospital (SSVH) at Subroto Park, New Delhi: This hospital was launched in October, 1996 and the following facilities have been provided for the welfare of ex-Servicemen and their families:

a) Haemodialysis centre.

b) Day care chemctheraphy.

c) ICU facilities.

d) IOL operations.

e) Operation theatre.

In addition, a cobolt radiotheraphy centre will also be established soon.

DIRECTORATE GENERAL OF DEFENCE ESTATE

The directorate General of Defence Estates is the apex body of the organisation having its offices in various parts of the country. It is entrusted with the task of administration of cantonments; the management of defence lands both inside and outside cantonments; acquisition, requisitioning and hiring of immovable properties for defence purposes and administration of urban land (Ceiling and Regulation) Act 1976 in 24 cantonments to which the Act applies.

The defence lands are situated in 62 cantonments as well

as outside including the camping grounds and abandoned airfields. Defence lands given for private use in the form of about 49,000 'Old Grant' sites and 3,500 leases for residential and other purposes are also managed by this department. To provide some relief to the Holders of Occupancy Rights (HOR) of old grant sites and other resumable tenures, the government has allowed additions, alterations, repairs, maintenance, reconstruction and renovation of buildings subject to certain conditions. Around 3,300 buildings have been hired for the residential and office accommodation of the defence forces. In addition, 79,395 acres of lands are held under hiring/requisitioning. There are also a large number of cases of acquisition/transfer of land for the defence purposes.

To assess the efficacy of the existing land management practices, a system of audit of defence land has been introduced. Focus has been cast on minimising fresh acquisition of land and optimising the existing land use for the benefit of defence forces. Management of the shopping complex known as 'Santushti' in New Delhi has also been entrusted to this department.

As part of the democratisation process, elections were held smoothly in 4 cantonments namely, Ambala, Ahmedabad, Mathura and Clementown on the expiry of the term of the elected members. Financial assistance by way of grant-in-aid to the tune of Rs. 22 crore has been allocated to meet the budgetary gap of the deficit cantonment boards. Development works such as water supply, maintenance of roads, street lighting, and so on in the cantonment areas gained momentum due to the release of service charge to the extent of Rs. 100 crore.

OFFICE OF THE CHIEF ADMINISTRATIVE OFFICER

The office of Chief Administrative Officer (CAO) is responsible for providing civilian manpower and infrastructural support to the services headquarters and the Headquarters offices of Inter-Services Organisations (ISOs) under the Ministry of Defence. The Joint Secretary (Training) also discharges the functions of the Chief Administrative Officer (CAO) and Director (Security). In relation to security, he oversees the work of the Chief

Security Officer. The functions of CAO's Office are discharged by the six divisions. The administration division provides administration cover to over 10,000 civilian manpower posted in army headquarters and ISOs.

The recommendations of the Vth Pay Commission in so far as related to pay and allowances were implemented by this division in a record time. The personnel division deals with the placement of civilian 9.2 personnel in the Service Headquarters and ISOs, their promotion and deputation outside the organisation. The recruitment division is responsible for framing policy on recruitment rules in consultation with DOP&T and effecting direct recruitment against all vacancies against civilian posts in the service headquarters and ISOs through prescribed channels. The finance and materials division provides material support which includes procuring and provisioning of office equipment, stores, furniture and stationery to all offices of army headquarters and ISOs.

The estates and Works Division performs estate function in respect of the defence pool residential accommodation to house senior defence officers posted to the headquarters. Presently, it manages 2,328 residential units and 257 hired houses. The upkeep and maintenance of office buildings is also undertaken by this division through CPWD. The training and welfare activities are looked after by the training, Coordination and Welfare Division.

For training purposes, a training institute functions under the training, Coordination and Welfare Division to impart induction training in office procedure and so on to fresh staff in clerical and stenographers streams. Other short-term courses of relevance to work being performed by civilian manpower including use of personal computers are also organised. Civilian officers are also sent to various training institutes spread all over India for training purposes.

The welfare of civilian employees in the service headquarters and Ministry of Defence is being looked after by this office. The armed forces headquarters/Inter-Services Organisations Welfare Fund and Defence Civilians Medical

Aid Fund (DCMAF) provide financial help to the employees during the hours of acute distress. The DCMAF, having all-India coverage, provides financial assistance in the cases of TB, cancer, leprosy, burn injuries, and so on to its members during the service. Its scope has now been enlarged to include post-retirement period also, if members opt for the same. The interest of women employees working in the Ministry of Defence is being looked after by the women's cell of the Ministry of Defence functioning under the Chairmanship of JS(Trg) & CAO.

The cell is presently helped by its 22 nodal women cells constituted in offices in the lower formations of the Ministry. Recently, in pursuance to the guidelines issued by the supreme court in their judgment in a case, a Complaints Committee has been constituted in this office to look into the complaints relating to sexual harassment of women employees at workplace. Besides, a Grievance Cell headed by an officer of director level also functions in this office to look after grievances of serving/retired civilian employees. During the current year up to November 1998, 387 grievance cases have been settled by this Cell.

Sports and cultural activities are also given a place of importance. Civilian employees are encouraged to join different sports activities. Every year, the sportspersons of this organisation participate in various competitions at different levels and win prizes for their organisation. Some of them even participate in national games and have the rare honour of representing the country in international meets. Recently, Shri Sukhminder Singh, an employee of AFHQ Cadre/ presently working in Air HQ, represented India In Master World Power Lifting Championship held at Cordoba; Argentina.

The office of CAO has been able to maintain its prime position in the Ministry of Defence for the past several years in the implementation of the official language policy of the government and progressive use of official language. This momentum has been maintained by celebrating 'Hindi Day, Hindi Pakhwara, Hindi Mas' and by organising several workshops on Raj Bhasha this year, apart from bringing out the fourth issue of the in-house Hindi magazine *Samvaad*. Chief Security officer and personnel under his command ensure the physical security of office building in the Defence Security Zone under the supervision of JS(Trg) & CAO. The security of buildings has to be ensured to preclude breach of physical security in the zone.

ARMY PURCHASE ORGANISATION

The army purchase Organisation (APO) in the Ministry of Defence is entrusted with the responsibility of the procurement and the timely supply of dry ration items for the consumption of the defence forces. The APO procures rice and wheat through the Food Corporation of India; sugar from the Directorate of Sugar; pulses, animal rations, edible oils, vanaspati, tea and Milk products from the central public sector undertakings like the State Trading Corporation and Hindustan Vegetable Oils Corporation Limited, state public sector undertakings like the Madhya Pradesh Export Corporation and Punjab State Civil Supplies Corporation and through the national cooperative federations like the National Cooperative Dairy Federation of India and the National Dairy Development Board and through various state level cooperative consumer federations.

Tinned items like vegetables, fruits, jellies and jams, tinned milk, meat and fish products, coffee, egg powder, and so on are procured from private parties through open tender. During the period under report, two new items, *i.e.*, cheese (tinned) and ghee have been introduced for procurement by APO. The indented quantities as per the army specifications are procured keeping in view the flush season of the items so as to ensure the cost-effective procurement. During the year 1998-1991 a budget provision of Rs. 690.78 crore was provided for procurement of the above items by this organisation. The quality control of the contracted items is ensured by the composite food laboratories under the charge of the army headquartes, who after inspection and commodities, the acceptance of the tenders supervise dispatches of the goods to different supply depots as per the dispatch instructions issued by the Army HQ.

HISTORY DIVISION

The History Division functions as the record and reference organisation of the Ministry of Defence and the Indian Armed Forces. It advises the Ministry of Defence and the service headquarters on matters relating to military history, heraldry and ceremonials.

It was established after the Second World War to compile and publish official history of the Indian Armed Forces during the Second World War. After the formation of Pakistan, it functioned as the Combined inter-Services Historical Section (India & Pakistan). The history of the armed forces in the Second World War has been brought out in 24 volumes. A historical section was established in 1953 to write the official history of military operations of Indian Armed Forces during the post-partition period and other books pretaining to military history, apart from serving as the custodian of the operational records of the three services.

The History of Operations in Jammu & Kashmir was the first assignment. The Historical Section was redesignated as the History Division on April 1, 1992. It has already brought out volumes on military history. Some more books are currently under preparation. During the period, over 4,500 operational records were received from the service headquarters, units and formations.

About 410 service officers and scholars visited the record room to consult records and seek guidance on research assignments relating to military history. Moreover, 300 written queries from the various units, scholars from India and abroad were received and answered by this division. The Herladic Cell of the History Division has been assisting the services headquarters and the Ministry of Defence in naming new establishments, designing crests, badges and coining suitable mottoes for units/formations.

Records of the Indian National Army and the Royal Indian Navy Mutiny kept in the History Division were transferred to the National Archives of India in August 1997.

SERVICES SPORTS CONTROL BOARD

The Services Sports Control Board is responsible for

conducting and coordinating various sports activities of the three defence services. During 1998-99, the performance of Services sportsmen at the national and international levels was quite encouraging. In the present day scenario, when sportsmen generally perform well only, when their efforts are compensated by material benefits, services sportsmen continued to maintain high morale in the true spirit of sportsmanship. The achievements of services sportsmen during the period under review are given below.

INTERNTIONAL EVENTS

Services sportsmen performed exceedingly well for the country at the XIII Asian Games held at Bangkok from December 6-20, 1998. In boxing PO NG Dingko Singh won the Gold Medal and Nb Sub Gurcharan Singh won the Bronze Medal. JWO Ram Mehar Singh and Hav Kiran Pal Singh represented the kabadi team which won the Gold Medal. In the team events for rowing, equestrian and shooting, Services sportsmen won Bronze medals. The following Services sportsmen won laurels at the Commonwealth Games held at Kualaumpur, Malaysia from September 11 to 21, 1998:

Weightlifting

POSTD D. Wilson	—	Individual	—	Gold Medal
		Overall	—	Silver Medal
Hav G. Vaidevelu	—	Individual	—	Bronze Medal

Shooting

MGPO Satinder Kumar	—	Silver Medal.
Nb Sub BL Dhaka	—	Bronze Medal.

At the Amir Temur Cup International Boxing tournament held at Uzbekistan from September 12 to 19, 1998, Spr Mangesh Kamble won the Silver Medal and Spr S. Selvaraj & Spr Bhagya Rajan won a Bronze Medal each. Spr Mangesh Kamble won the Bronze Medal at the 9th Asian Youth Boxing Championship held at Kausiung, Taiwan, from August 14 to 22, 1998. Nb Sub Gurcharang Singh won the Gold Medal and CPO N.G. Dingko Singh won the Silver Medal at the training-cum-competition of Indian boxing squad held at Cuba from May 19 to June 17, 1998.

NATIONAL EVENTS

Services teams won the senior and junior National Kayaking and Canoeing Championship, Junior National Rowing Championship, Junior National Boxing Championship, Gold Medal in the National Handball Championship, secured second position in Diving and third position in swimming and water polo at the Senior National Equatics Championships, second position in the National Squash Championship, third position in the National Volleyball Championship. The services sportsmen won a Silver and a Bronze Medal (Black Belt Category) and a Bronze Medal at the National Taekwondo Championship.

SCHOOL OF FOREIGN LANGUAGES

The school of Foreign Languages, established in 1948, has been a pioneer in fosreign language teaching in India. At present, the school is engaged in imparting, training in ten foreign languages to personnel of the three services and government departments. The languages taught are Arabic, Bahasa Indonesia, Burmese, Chinese, French, German, Russian, Spanish, Sinhala and Tibetan. It also caters to the needs of the Ministry of External Affairs and the Cabinet Secretariat, and so on.

The courses offered by the SFL are as follows:

i) Interpretership Course.

ii) Certificate of Proficiency Course.

iii) Advance Diploma (Intensive) Course.

iv) Short-term/capsule Courses

Officials are sponsored by the Ministry of Defence, the Cabinet Secretariat and other government departments for the full-time Interpretership Course which trains them to become experts in the highly skilled work of interpretation and translation. The duration of the Interpretership Course ranges from 16-1/2 months to 23-1/2 months and has been designed solely to meet the specific needs of the armed forces. The Certificate of Proficiency Course and the Advanced Diploma Intensive Course are part-time courses, each of one-year duration. Together, these two courses are equivalent to the three-year diploma courses of the universities. Short-term courses are purely need-based programmes. They are conducted as and when necessary, especially for Military Attache Designates and officers being sent on UN missions.

The SFL is responsible for framing the standard and syllabus for the foreign language examinations conducted by the Ministry of External Affairs; the National Defence Academy, Pune; the Army Education Centre and Training College, Pachmarhi; the Cabinet Secretariat and the Ministry of Home Affairs. It conducts their examinations and issues diplomas to the successful candidates.

NATIONAL DEFENCE COLLAGE (NDC)

The National Defence College (NDC), inaugurated on April 27, 1960, is the only institution in the country that imparts knowledge on all aspects of national security and strategy. the senior defence and civil service officers participate in a 47-weeks comprehensive programme of national security and strategy. The training at NDC is highly specialised to equip the participants with future planning of national strategy in the context of world polity.

The NDC alumni have risen to the highest military posts in countries like Sri Lanka, Australia and Malaysia. The 38th NDC Course concluded on December 2, 1998. Officers numbering from army, navy, air force and friendly foreign countries participated in it. A total of 160 experts on various subjects were invited to speak to course members of 38th NDC course. The following seven studies were conducted during the 38th NDC course:

a) Socio-political study of India.

b) Economy, science and technology.

c) International security environment.

d) Global issues.

e) India's strategic neighbourhood.

f) India's immediate neighbourhood.

g) Strategies and structures for national security.

As part of the course curriculum, student officers visited 13 countries *viz.*, Turkey, Vietnam, Nigeria, France, Egypt,

Mauritius, Israel, Greece, and SAARC countries—Nepal, Bhutan, Bangladesh, Sri Lanka and Maldives. Commandant, NDC and Senior Directing Staff (FS) also attended the 2nd Asia Regional Forum meeting of the heads of defence colleges/institutions held in Seoul from November 7 to 11, 1998. Delegations from Bangladesh, USA, Kenya, Poland, South Africa, and Vietnam visited NDC during 1998.

ARMED FORCES FILM $ PHOTO DIVISION (AFFPD)

Production, procurement and distribution of training films, production of photographs, art work, and so on to meet the needs of training, weapon trials, security, defence research, intelligence records and photo and video coverage of ceremonial functions of the Ministry of Defence is the responsibility of the Armed Forces Film and Photo Division (AFFPD). Training films of classified and specialised nature are produced by AFFPD themselves. Some unclassified films are also made through Films Division, Ministry of Information and Broadcasting. Six training films were produced till December 98. Work on ten defence training films is under progress.

AFFPD has a very rich collection of rare films and photographs looking back into the history. This material, inherited from the British after Independence, is of historical value. The photographs depict the Indian forces in action in the various theatres during World War-II. The Armed Forces Film and Photo Division (AFFPD) has a Central Defence Film Library and a Mobile Cinema Unit. The Central Defence Film Library of this division, responsible for distribution of training films to various units/formations/training establishments/commands to meet their specific training requirements/schedules, holds 595 titles in 35mm sizes, 1,710 in 16mm sizes, 315 in Video format and 370 filmstrips. During the year, 990 training films/video cassettes were distributed. A total of 5,842 photographs/slides were made and 1,856 pieces of artwork prepared.

The Mobile Cinema Unit distributes documentary films/ news magazines containing information on cultural aspects, general knowledge, family welfare aspects and so on to the troops in the forward areas. As a special assignment, this division is providing technical advice and photographic resources to Directorate General of Signals (ISTT) in connection with the preparation of a pictorial coffee table book based on updated history and hi-tech achievements of the Corps of Signals. A large number of professionally shot photographs and transparencies have been made by deploying several photo teams to conduct photography involving typical signals activities under various terrains/ operational/training conditions.

DIRECTORATE OF PUBLIC RELATIONS

Media management for clear communication has assumed great importance, with India's entry into the nuclear power arena. The Directorate of Public Relations is entrusted with this responsibility of providing the media support for the Ministry of Defence. The Department of Public Relations has its headquarters in Delhi and 24 offices spread across the country. The officers of the Indian Information Service and specially selected officers from the three services man the directorate. During the crucial phase of India's transformation from the non-nuclear weapon state to the nuclear weapon state, the communication lifeline in national and international fora was managed by the DPR by arranging multi-media conferences. The nuclear tests in May 1998 marked the advent of a new facet to India's defence prepardness.

These developments were given due publicity throughtout the media conference arranged for the specific purpose, attended by national and international media representatives, and was jointly addressed by the Scientific Advisor to the Defence Minister and the Chairman of the Atomic Energy Commission. The media was also taken to Pokhran for a spot visit. The photo section is an important publicity unit of the directorate with its eight units attached to the regional units of DPR.

The unit supplied over 700 photographs to the print media including the *Sainik Samachar*, focussing different defence-related events. The Broadcasting Section of the Directorate maintained a close liaison with All India Radio and arranged broadcast for various entertaining and informative programmes for the armed forces. At the headquarters, more than 500 press releases were issued; over 40 press conferences were organised for the Defence Minister and other senior officers to project the ministry's point of view. Besides, a series of special briefings were arranged. A number of media parties were conducted at various locations and defence establishments to focus on important issues.

Notable among other events publicised during the year 1998 include the Defence Minister's visit to Siachen and Aero India-98 show. A media team accompanied the Minister on his road journey to Siachen, and on another occasion, officials of the directorate went with him to ensure wide publicity in both print as well as the visual media. The international air show in Bangalore was extensively publicised through our media management and supervision.

The revival of the Defence Minister's Committee, after a gap of more than 20 years, enabling the three service chiefs to participate in decision-making quickly and more effectively; a substantial increase of Siachen allowance for the armed forces personnel and also the announcement of various welfare measures for the officers, JCOs and other ranks of the services were all given maximum publicity. The Defence Minister's visits to major defence locations in difficult areas from the hills and forests of the north-east, the snow-bound mountains of Jammu and Kashmir, the deserts of Rajasthan, the Rann of Kutch and the choppy waters of Andamans were publicised in the media whereby the general public was kept well informed, suitable publicity was arranged for dignitaries from China, United States, Russia, Greece and other countries who called on the Defence Minister. The year 1998 witnessed the appointment of the new Chief of Naval Staff and thc new Chief of Air Staff. Admiral Sushil Kumar took over as the Chief of Naval Staff, while Air Chief Marshal AY Tipnis as the Chief of Air Staff. The events were widely covered by electronic as well as print media.

Following the decision by cabinet committee on security, the Indian navy opened all its branches for women officers.

Till then women were only eligible for induction into the support branches and cadres of the navy. The naval version of the Advanced Light Helicopter (ALH) developed by the Hindustan Aeronautics Limited (HAL), Bangalore, was successfully launched from the aircraft carrier INS Virat and indigenously built *INS Ganga* off the Western Seaboard in March 1998.

Publicity was arranged for these achievements of the Indian navy. *Trishul*, the biggest operational exercise of the Indian Air Force conducted by Western Air Command in March-April 1998 was also given wide publicity. The media was taken with the army chief during his visits to forward areas including Poonch and Rajouri sector in Jammu & Kashmir, Assam and Arunachal Pradesh in the north-east. The three services provided assistance to civil authorities during the Malpa avalanche tragedy and floods in West Bengal, Bihar and UP. This was given due publicity through the media. Achievements of the defence public sector undertakings including Bharat Electronics Limited, Mazagon Dock and Garden Reach Shipbuilders & Engineers were suitably publicised. Notable among these was the commissioning of India's Extra Fast Attack Craft produced by Goa Shipyards Limited.

Necessary media coverage was arranged for the Indian delegation led by Defence Secretary who visited Russia in June 1998, and for the Indo-Pak Secretary level talks. A press conference arranged after the Secretary-level talks and addressed among others by the Defence Secretary and Director General of Military Operations, was attended by both Indian and foreign media persons. A new contract was finalised for printing and despatching *Sainik Samachar*.

The magazine was published regularly during the year. Copies of the journal being published in 13 languages—English Assamese, Bengali, Gorkhali, Hindi/ Kannada, Malayalam, Marathi, Oriya, Punjabi, Tamil, Telugu and Urdu—were sent to the field units of the three wings of the Services also, besides the regular subscribers.

Suitable publicity was arranged during the period under review for various recurring events like the Republic Day celebrations, Independence Day celebrations, Investiture Ceremonies, Army Day, Navy Day, Air Force Day, Vijay Divas, NCC Day and Raising Days of different formations of the three services and inter services organisations.

MINISTRY OF DEFENCE LIBRARY

The Ministry of Defence Library, a central defence library, provides literature on relevant subjects to officials responsible for planning and policy formulation in the Ministry of Defence, the three services headquarters, inter-services organisations and other allied defence establishments located in Delhi. During the year, the library added 731 books, subscribed 137 journals and 24 newspapers.

The library at present holds approximately 50,000 books. It specialises in defence and related subjects, besides catering to the needs of a general reading clientele. Besides 450 photocopies of articles circulated to senior officers by way of SDI/RSD services, the library issues three bulletins periodically on new additions—books, articles from journals/ newspapers. The reading material for the library is selected by a Book Selection Sub-Committee constituted by the Ministry of Defence.

DEFENCE SERVICES STAFF COLLAGE (DSSC)

The Defence Services Staff College is one of the oldest military training institutions which was established in 1905 in Deolah and has been functioning at Wellington since 1958. The Defence Services Staff College imparts training to middle level officers of the three services besides a few civilian officers and officers from friendly foreign countries.

The college conducts a 45-weeks training programme from June to April every year. During 1998-99, 29 officers from friendly foreign countries attended the 55th Staff Course. The Staff Course at DSSC aims at imparting training in operational and staff functions in an inter-service and joint-service environment. The training enables the officers to perform effectively any staff/ operational appointments as Maj /Lt Col and equivalent ranks in other services.

COLLAGE DEFENCE MANAGEMENT

The Institute of Defence Management, Secunderabad, established in June 1970, was renamed as the College of Defence Management (CDM) in 1980. The CDM conducts training programmes oriented towards the application of management concept and techniques to defence situations in all facets—operations, logistics, intelligence and training. The prominent training programmes conducted by the CDM are Long Defence Management Course, Senior Defence Management Course, Defence Management Seminar and Assignment Oriented Management Training Programme.

11

Recruitment and Training

Recruitment to the armed forces is voluntary, and every citizen of India, irrespective of his caste, class, religion and community, is eligible for recruitment into the armed forces provided he meets the laid down physical, medical and educational criteria. Recruitment into the army is carried out according to Recruitable Male Population (RMP) of each state.

Recruitment of Officers

Recruitment of Commissioned Officers in the armed forces is mainly through the Union Public Service Commission (UPSC). For technical branches, recruitment is made directly through the Service Selection Boards for the army and navy and through the Air Force Selection Board for the air force.

Recruitment through UPSC

UPSC holds an all-India competitive examination, known as the Combined Defence Services Examination (CDSE), twice a year. University graduates are eligible to appear in the examination. On an average, about 1.7 lakh candidates appear in the UPSC examination and the UPSC recommends about 13-14 thousand candidates every year. However, many candidates are rejected at the Service Selection Boards (SSBs) level. Successful candidates join the respective training academies, *viz*., the Indian Military Academy (IMA) for the army, the naval academy for the navy and the air force.

Academy for the air force. The UPSC also holds an examination for entry into the National Defence Academy

(NDA) twice a year. Candidates on completion of the 10+2 examination or while in the 12th standard are eligible to compete in this examination. Successful candidates thereafter join the NDA.

UNIVERSITY ENTRY SCHEME

Final/pre-final year students in engineering disciplines are eligible for induction into the technical branches/services of the army, as Commissioned Officers under the University Entry Scheme.

SHORT SERVICE COMMISSION ENTRY SCHEME

To alleviate the shortage of Technical Officers (Engineering) in the army, the government has approved the Short Service Commission (Technical) Entry Scheme. This envisages recruitment of qualified technical graduates through the SSBs, to attend the Officers Training Academy (OTA), Madras, after medical tests, for a 10-month course. On completion of training at the OTA, successful candidates are inducted as Short Service Commissioned Officers in the technical branches of the army.

RECRUITMENT OF MEDICAL OFFICERS

Medical graduates from the Armed Forces Medical College, Pune, are directly inducted as permanent Commissioned Medical Officers in the armed forces. For recruitment of Regular Commissioned/ Short Service Commissioned Medical Officers from the graduates/postgraduates of Civil Medical Colleges, the Director General of the Armed Forces Medical Services conducts an all-India competitive examination.

RECRUITMENT OF WOMEN OFFICERS

Eligible women are recruited as officers on Short Service Commission basis in the following branches of the Armed Forces.

Recruitment through NCC

University graduates possessing NCC 'C' Certificate with minimum 'B' grading and 50 per cent marks in graduation are inducted in the navy and air force as Regular Commissioned Officers, and as Short Service Commission officers in the army. These graduates are exempted from appearing in the CDSE conducted by the UPSC and are selected through the SSBs.

Induction under Special Commissioned Officer Scheme

The government has approved the creation of a 6,000 strong support cadre of Special Commmissional Officers. These posts will be filled up by eligible Cos and OR. Under this entry, serving JCOs/NCOs/OR in the age group of 30-35 years, with an Army Senior School Certificate Pass (Class XI CBSE Pattern) qualification, will be eligible for commission affair screening/selection through the Service Selection Board and a Medical Board.

They will undergo a pre-commission training of six months duration. The officers so commissioned will earn promotion and the acting rank of Colonel. The rules for substansive promotion and acting promotion will be the same as for regular officers. These officers will be employed in units as subunit Cadres/QM job/ERE appointments and so on, up to the rank of Major. They will be retire at the age of 57 years after serving about 20-25 years as officers. The scheme will not only improve the career prospects of the existing JCOs/NCOs/OR but will also help in making up the deficiency of the officers in the army to a considerable extent.

10 + 2 technical entry scheme

Under this scheme candidates with 10 + 2 qualification, after selection through will be sent for military and engineering training, at IMA and the College of Military Training, Pune, for initial six months engineer followed by degree military training of 4 years. This scheme will help in bringing down the deficiency of officers in technical arms/services.

RECRUITMENT OF OTHER RANKS (OR)

Recruitment to the army is carried out according to the Recruitable Male Population (RMP) of each state. The RMP of the male of a state is reckoned to be 10 per cent of the male population of the state.

The recruitment demands are projected to army headquarters by Naval Head Recruitment, of airmen to the air force Central Airmen Selection Board located at the Air Force Station, New Delhi.

RECRUITMENT OF JAWANS THROUGH OPEN RECRUITMENT RALLIES

A new system of recruitment has been introduced with effect from April 1, 1998. Under the revised system, recruitment of the jawans in the army has carried out through open recruitment rallies only. Recruitment rallies are planned well in advance keeping in view the geographical, demographical, topographical considerations. At least one such rally is held in each month, combining districts areas and regions, depending upon the response anticipated, thereby giving every aspirant, irrespective of his place for residence, at least one opportunity in a year to get himself enrolled in the army.

In the old system of Branch Recruiting Office-oriented recruitment, aspirants had to transverse long distances to reach the nearest BRO for enrolment, whereas in the revised system, recruitment has been brought closer to the domiciles. Advance publicity regarding an ensuing rally in a particular area/ district is given by putting up hoardings, advertisements in local newspapers, radio and so on.

DISPENSATIONS IN EDUCATIONAL STANDARDS

For recruitment of general duty (GD) category soldiers in the Indian army, the prescribed minimum educational qualification is Matric/SSLC. To facilitate representations in the army of people from remote, border, hilly and backward areas, certain dispensations in educational qualifications, valid up to March 31, 2001 have been given.

DISPENSATIONS FROM CLASS X TO CLASS VIII

These are enunciated below:

i) *Jammu& Kashmir*: The whole state of J&K (except Ladakh region and Samba and Kathua districts of Jammu region).

ii) *Uttar Pradesh*: All personnel from the border tehsils of Uttarkashi district (Bhatwari Tehsil), Okhimath and Joshimath tehsils of Chamoli District and Didihat, Dharchula and Munsiari tehsils of Pithoragarh District.

iii) *Rajasthan*: All personnel from the border districts of Jaisalmer, Barmer and Shergarh, Osian and Phelodi tehsils of Jodhpur District.

iv) *Gujarat*: All personnel from Rapar and Lakhpat tehsils of Kutch.

v) *Sikkim*: All personnel from Sikkim state.

vi) *Lakshadweep and Minicoy Group of Islands*: All inhabitants of Lakshadweep and Minicoy Group of Islands.

vii) *Andaman and Nicobar Group of Islands*: All inhabitants of Andaman and Nicobar Group of Islands.

viii) Class/Community-wise dispensations are provided to all Nepalese and Indian-domiciled Gorkhas, Kiam-Khanis; from Rajasthan, and Mahars from Maharashtra, Andhra Pradesh, Madhya Pradesh and Karnataka, and Rawat community from Ajmer, Rajasmad, Bhilwara, Udaipur & Chittor Districts of Rajasthan.

ix) All personnel from Assam, Manipur, Mizoram, Nagaland and Tripura (except tribals from these states).

Dispensation from Class X to Class V pass has been given to all personnel from Arunachal Pradesh, Meghalaya, Lahaul, Spiti and Kinnaur districts of Himachal Pradesh and tribals from all the states. Dispensation to be literate in their own language is provided for all personnel from Ladakh region of Jammu and Kashmir. The rules also provide for relaxation in prescribed physical standards in respect of certain specified backward, remote and tribal regions. Relaxation in physical standards is also given to one son and one grandson of serving or retired soldiers and widows of battle casualties.

PUBLICITY FOR RECRUITMENT

Measures have been taken to make the youth of our country more aware of the opportunities in the army, both for officers including women officers and other Rank categories. The means of publicity adopted to attract better talent are as follows:

Press advertisements

Advertisements are released through the Directorate of

Advertising and Visual Publicity (DAVP) in the *Employment News/Rozgar Samachar* and in newspapers in different languages for various entries *viz.*, National Defence Academy, Combined Defence Services Examination, Technical Graduate Course, Short Service Commission (Technical & Non-Technical), University Entry Scheme, Law Graduates, Induction in Medical Services for both men and women, Special Entry Scheme (officers), Havildar Instructors, Junior Commissioned Officers (catering and religious teachers) and so on, which are covered in these newspapers. A composite advertisement on various entries in the army is also brought out periodically both in English and Hindi. Concerned Zonal Recruitment Offices (ZROs)/ Branch Recruitment Offices (BROs) also publish advertisements on recruitment of other ranks in local regional newspapers.

Advertisements in journals/magazines

These are normally brought out in the journals of educational institutions.

Hoardings

Hoardings are erected at ZRO/BRO premises as well as adjacent to engineering colleges all over the country to attract technical talents into the army. The DAVP approves the sites and thereafter, the hoardings giving detailed information are Installed and maintained by them.

Printed publicity

Information folders, leaflets, brochures, data cards, posters and blow-ups, mostly prepared through DAVP, are widely distributed.

At the Defence pavilion at the India International Trade Fair, New Delhi, a stall is established where recruiting information is provided to visitors, each year. This is also done in other organised fairs, which are career oriented and meant for students.

IMAGE PROJECTION CAMPAIGN

Analysis of the shortage of quality personnel applying for commission in the army indicated that there is very poor awareness of the opportunities that are available on commissioning in the army. An advertising campaign was launched on September 6, 1997 with the assistance of a professional advertising agency to project positive aspects of a wholesome career available in the services.

The aim of the campaign was to reach out to every corner of the country through the print, audio, visual and audio-visual media. An evaluation check of the impact of the campaign was entrusted to an independent market research agency MODE. Their report has revealed that the campaign is working in the desired direction.

In the baseline study prior to the launch of the campaign, the army stood seventh in the list of careers spontaneously mentioned; this has improved to the fifth position going, by the feedback received from the research findings.

ENHANCEMENT IN RETIREMENT AGE OF DEFENCE PERSONNEL

The age of retirement of all defence personnel has been enhanced by two years, except that of Naval officers, officers of the army Medical Corps, Army Dental Corps, Military Nursing Service and Remount Veterinary Corps. Enhancement of retirement age of these personnel is under consideration of the government.

TRAINING

Training aims to equip the soldier with necessary inputs to make him not only an efficient fighting man, but also extremely well informed about national and international developments, both past and present. The specialised and rigorous recruitment procedures, the environment in which the defence officers have to interact, demand a holistic integrated approach to training. The requirements have to be properly matched for the freshly recruited officer, for those already in service for their advanced and specialised training, and Other Ranks (OR) as well.

SAINIK SCHOOLS

A scheme to establish Sainik Schools was started in 1961 to broadbase the recruitment of the officers cadre of the defence forces. Sainik Schools are joint ventures of the state and central governments. At present, 18 Sainik Schools, one each in all major states, are managed by the Sainik Schools Society. Boys from the states which do not have Sainik Schools, are admitted in Sainik Schools located in adjoining states.

Sainik Schools are fully residential schools and admit students to Classes VI and IX strictly in order of merit obtained in the All India Sainik Schools Entrance Examination held in February each year. These schools are affiliated to the Central Board of Secondary Education. All Sainik Schools are members of the Indian Public School Conference. In addition to grants-in-aid provided by the state governments, the day-to-day expenses for running the Sainik Schools are met from the tuition fee charged at the rate of Rs. 14,000/- per annum per student. It is proposed to revise the tuition fee to meet the increase in expenses. State governments and the Ministry of Defence provide a number of merit-cum-means scholarships to the students studying in Sainik Schools.

To motivate Sainik School students to join the National Defence Academy, the environment in Sainik Schools is geared for all-round personality development through P.T., sports & games, adventure activities, cultural activities, quiz competitions and defence establishments. Cadets of Sainik School regularly attended rock climbing courses, mountaineering courses and undertook cycling expeditions covering long distances.

The pass percentage of Sainik School students in Classes X and XII CBSE examinations, during the academic session 1997-98, was 99.5 per cent and 87.1 per cent respectively. Sainik School numbering 132 joined the national Defence Academy in 1998. Since their inception, Sainik Schools have contributed a total of 5,033 students to the National Defence Academy.

MILITARY SCHOOLS

There are five Military Schools in the country at Chail, Dholpur, Belgaum, Bangalore and Ajmer. They admit boys to Class VI based on an All India Entrance Examination. In Military Schools, 67 per cent vacancies are reserved for the wards of Personnel Below Officers Rank (PBOR), 20 per cent for the wards of service officers, and 13 per cent for the wards of civilians The aim of these schools is to impart quality education to enable the boys to take the All India Secondary School Examination and Senior Secondary Certificate Examination conducted by the CBSE, and also to facilitate their entry into the NDA.

RASHTRIYA INDIAN MILITARY COLLAGE (RIMC), DEHRADUN

This collage was established in March 1922 to provide necessary preliminary training to the boys, while studying in school, to become officers in the armed forces. The college admits students purely on merit basis in Class VIII through a written examination-cum-viva voce test under the aegis of the state governments throughout India twice every year in February and August. The students are provided education on the lines of residential public schools up to Class XII. Approximately 75 per cent to 80 per cent of RIMC students join NDA after competing in the examination conducted by the UPSC.

NATIONAL DEFENCE ACADEMY (NDA) KHADAGVASALA

The National Defence Academy (NDA) is a premier joint services training institution. It imparts academic as well as basic service training. On passing out from NDA, cadets are awarded BA or BSc degree of the Jawaharlal Nehru University. The academy is a unique institution wherein inter-service aspects are developed in the formative stages of an officer, thus, developing a bond of friendship and respect for each other's service. After passing out from NDA, the cadets go to their respective services/academies for specialised training before being commissioned in the armed forces. At present, there are 1,969 cadets undergoing training at the NDA, including 68 cadets from Bhutan, six cadets from Palestine and one cadet from the Maldives.

The NDA celebrated its 50th anniversary during February 19-21, 1999. The Vice President of India was the chief guest for the celebrations. To commemorate the event, NDA has undertaken a number of adventure activities including mountaineering, white water river rafting and a car rally.

INDIAN MILITARY ACADEMY (IMA), DEHRADUN

The Indian Military Academy (IMA) was established in 1932. The IMA trains Gentlemen Cadets (GCs) for commission into the Army. The various modes of entry into IMA are:

a) On graduation from NDA.
b) On graduation from Army Cadet College, which is a wing of the IMA itself.
c) Direct entry graduate cadets, who join on qualifying in the Union Public Service Commission Examination and the Services Selection Board.
d) Technical graduates.
e) University Entry Scheme for engineering college students in final/pre-final year studies.

The IMA also imparts training to gentlemen cadets from friendly countries like the Maldives, Mauritius, Seychelles, Sri Lanka, Nepal and Bhutan.

The present strength in IMA is 1558 gentlemen cadets which include 27 gentlemen cadets from Bhutan, 5 cadets from Palestine and 30 cadets from Sri Lanka, 1 cadet from the maldives and 1 cadet from Nepal. The IMA has another wing known as Army Cadet College (ACC) which caters for training of service cadets selected for commission.

The academic format is similar to the NDA on the lines of 10+2+3 and the syllabus is also common. On completion of the course, these cadets also qualify for a BA or BSc degree, recognised by the Jawaharlal Nehru University. The first Special Commissioned Officer (SCO) Course was conducted at IMA with effect from February 1998, and 161 GCs were imparted training. SCO-2 and SCO-3 commenced their training with effect from January 14, 1999.

OFFICERS TRAINING ACADEMY (OTA), CHENNAI

The Officers Training Academy was established in 1963 as an Officers Training School to meet the increased demand of officers in the army. It was redesignated as Officers Training Academy (OTA) from January 1, 1988 on completion of 25 years of its existence.

To begin with, its main task was to train gentlemen cadets for grant of Emergency Commission, and from 1965 onwards, the academy started training cadets for short service commission, after which the former commission was dispensed with. Since September 21,1992, the Indian Army has opened up its portals for entry of women as commissioned officers.

Initially, 50 lady cadets were commissioned every year with the entries presently limited to Army Service Corps, Army Ordnance Corps, Army Education Corps, Judge Advocate General's Department, Corps of Engineers, Signals, and Electrical and Mechanical Engineers. The strength of lady cadets from March 1997 course has been enhanced to 50 per course *i.e.*, 100 per year.

The OTA imparts pre-commission training for the following courses:

S.No	*Type of course*	*Education qualification*
1.	Short Service Commission	Graduation (Non-Technical)
2.	Short Service Commission	University Graduation in Engg. (Technical)
3.	Women's Special Entry Scheme	Graduate/ Post Graduate

In addition, the OTA conducts orientation training for selected service personnel for grant of Permanent Commission (Special List) as Technical and Records Officers. At present 506 GCs are under training at OTA.

COLLEGE OF COMBAT, MHOW

This college was established on April 1, 1971. It is the premier all arms tactical training institution for officers and performs the important functions of evaluation of new concepts and doctrines in the fields of tactics and logistics. The college imparts training to officers of all arms and services at various levels of command *viz.*, sub unit (junior command), unit (senior command) and formation (higher command). Inter-arms and inter-services aspects are included in the training which is aimed at enabling officers to handle mixed groups of various arms and services at levels appropriate to the course.

Officers from Paramilitary organisations are also allotted vacancies on the senior command (13 weeks) and the junior command (13 weeks) courses. In addition, officers from friendly foreign countries also attend these courses. The higher command course (45 weeks) is restricted to the officers of the Indian army, navy and air force only. Besides the above courses, a new four weeks course named the Formation Commanders Orientation Programme was started in 1996 for Brigadiers approved for the rank of Major General.

The aim of the course is to prepare selected potential divisional commanders for command of their formations in field and peace. Another capsule called the Combined Operational Review and Evaluation Programme is conducted for officers of the rank of Major Generals and equivalent from all the three services. The aim of this programme is to update the general officers in the geostatic and geopolitical environment.

DEFENCE SERVICES STAFF COLLEGE (DSSC)

The Defence Services Staff College is one of the oldest military institutions, which was established in 1905 in Deolali and has been functioning at Wellington since 1950. The Defence Services Staff College imparts training to middle level officers of the three services besides a few civilian officers and officers from friendly foreign countries. The college conducts a 45-week training programme from June to April every year.

During 1998-99, 29 officers from friendly foreign countries attended the 55th Staff Course. The Staff Course at DSSC aims at imparting training in operational and staff functions in an inter-service and joint-service environment. The training enables the officers to perform effectively any staff/operational appointments as Maj/Lt Col and equivalent ranks in other services.

HIGH ALTITUDE WARFARE SCHOOL

The High Altitude Warfare School (HAWS), in its present form, was established in April 1962. The school is commanded by a Brigadier and imparts training in high altitude mountain and winter warfare to officers, JCOs and NCOs of the Indian army and some friendly foreign countries. The following courses are conducted at HAWS:

a) Winter Warfare Basic Course.
b) Winter Warfare Advance Course.
c) Mountain Warfare Course.
d) Mountain Warfare Advance Course.

The HAWS has the distinction of being the only training establishment which has taken part both in 1965 and 1971 wars, besides Low Intensity Conflict Operations in J & K in their close vicinity. The school contributes tremendously towards preparing troops operations in Siachen Glacier, the highest battlefield in the world, and other high altitude areas. The institution is operationally active.

Expert teams were provided for opening four land routes in the Siachen Glacier so that troops could be kept supplied even when air supply failed. A number of mountain rescue teams have been trained so that the units are self-sufficient in dealing with emergency situations. An international skiing tournament was held in 1998 at Gulmarg under the aegis the HAWS which has brought India on the map of Winter Games.

COUNTER INSURGENCY & JUNGLE WARFARE SCHOOLS (CIJW)

The Counter Insurgency & Jungle Warfare School (CIJW), in its present form, was established on May 1, 1970, as Category 'A' Establishment and located at Veirengte, Mizoram. The school motto 'Fight the Guerilla like a Guerilla' is unique and symbolic of the CIJW techniques. The school is currently training officers and men in fighting Low Intensity Conflict Operations (LICO). The following courses are conducted at CIJW School:

a) Low Intensity Combat Courses.
b) Language courses for JCOs/NCOs in Nagamese, Manipuri and Tangkhul.

A number of students from paramilitary forces and friendly foreign countries like Sri Lanka, Nepal, Singapore, Kenya, Iraq, USA also attend the above courses. Seven officers from foreign countries attended the courses in 1998. The CIJW is training 120 officers, 460 JCOs/NCOs and giving pre-induction training to companies of paramilitary forces. CIJW has also done well in looking after the interests of tribal villages in its close vicinity by establishing a junior school, which has become very popular all over.

INFANTRY SCHOOLS, MHOW

The Infantry School is the largest and the oldest military training institution of the Indian army. The origin of the institution can be traced back to the year 1885. The present Infantry School owes its origin to a decision taken shortly after Independence to amalgamate the country's various tactical and weapons training institutions into one single school of instructions at Mhow.

The School is responsible for:

a) Developing new tactical doctrine battle techniques and battle drills pertaining to infantry and introducing them after approval of the army headquarters.

b) Continuous study and keeping abreast of tactical and technical development in India and abroad in all matters pertaining to functions of the school.

c) Carrying out trials of weapons, equipment and ammunition pertaining to the infantry as ordered by the army headquarters.

d) Conducting courses of instructions.

e) Training the army shooting team and the national shooting team in "precision shooting".

The Infantry School is located in two places. The Weapons Wing and Young Officers Wing are located at Mhow. The Junior Leaders Wing consisting of Commando Platoon Commanders Wing is located at Belgaum. The institution is training Officers, JCOs and OR of not only infantry but other arms and services also besides paramilitary forces and civil police organisations.

A number of friendly foreign countries are making use of the facilities and in 1998, 90 officers and 160 JCOs/NCOs from friendly foreign countries are attended the courses.

With the above backdrop, the institution is currently training 1,195 officers and 5,900 JCOs/NCOs in a year. The Army Marksmanship Unit at Infantry School has produced excellent results at national and international level.

COLLEGE OF DEFENCE MANAGEMENT

The Institute of Defence Management, Secunderabad, established in June 1970, was renamed as the College of Defence Management (CDM) in 1980. The CDM conducts training programmes oriented towards the application of management concept and techniques to defence situations in all facets—operations, logistics, intelligence and training. The prominent training programmes conducted by the CDM are Long Defence Management Course, Senior Defence Management Course, Defence Management Seminar and Assignment Oriented Management Training Programme. The college also undertakes management consultancy studies.

MILITARY MUSIC

Training is imparted regularly to military bands at the Military Music Wing of Army Educational Corps Training College at Pachmarhi. A number of courses, ranging from one year to three years, are being run at the Military Music Wing. Vacancies are also allotted to personnel of Paramilitary forces and students from friendly countries. The Military Music Wing of AEC Training College at Pachmarhi is the only institute of its kind in Asia.

INDIAN MILITARY BAND

The performance of the Combined Services band that played at a function to commemorate Vijay Diwas in Delhi has been included in the Guinness Book of Records for 1998. The event, which coincided with the 50th Anniversary of India's Independence, was held at Vijay Chowk. Thirty-six military bands and 251 pipes & drums from the army including two from the navy and four from the air force had taken part in the record-breaking feat. The Combined Services band, comprising 227 pipes, 902 drums, 258 buglers and 937 brass band personnel, besides 135 band majors, had a strength of 4,459 musicians and had performed amazing grace under one army conductor.

ARMY ADVENTURE WING

The Army Adventure Wing conducts and supports various forms of adventure activities keeping in view the following:

a) Expose army personnel to high risk training activities so that they take correct decisions under pressure.

b) Develop a spirit of camaraderie amongst volunteers.

c) Develop administrative skills while handling difficult situations.

d) Enhance self-confidence of team members.

e) Inculcate leadership qualities in army personnel.

12

Welfare of Ex-Servicemen

About 60,000 service personnel are retired/released each year. A majority of ex-servicemen prefer to settle down near their home towns after their release from the services. Accordingly, resettlement and welfare of ex-servicemen has been accepted as a joint responsibility of the central as well as the state governments.

Both the central and state governments have introduced a number of schemes for the welfare of ex-servicemen, and to provide them rehabilitation through re-employment in the organised sector or through self-employment. The benefits extended to ex-servicemen and their dependants vary from state to state.

The Ex-Servicemen Welfare Wing of the Ministry of Defence is responsible for the formulation of the policy guidelines and schemes for resettlement of ex-servicemen at the centre. The Director General of Resettlement (DGR), under the Ministry of Defence (MOD), is the nodal agency for overseeing execution and proper implementation of the central schemes for ex-servicemen.

The DGR is also responsible for liaison with the state/UT governments. In the states and union territories, the Departments of Sainik Welfare at the state level and Zila Sainik Welfare offices at the district level are functioning to attend to the problems of ex-servicemen and to execute the rehabilitation and welfare schemes at the state and district levels respectively.

Ex-Servicemen Population

A total of 14,53,013 ex-servicemen and 2,74,632 widows of

the service personnel were registered with various Zila Sainik Boards in the country as on June 30, 1998. The ex-servicemen population is mainly concentrated in the states of Uttar Pradesh (2,53,644), Punjab (1,80,539), Haryana (1,46,155), Maharashtra (1,30,397), Kerala (1,21,965), Tamil Nadu (99,746), Rajasthan (94,460) and Himachal Pradesh (73,981).

RESETTLEMENT

Efforts are constantly on to explore various avenues for employment of ex-servicemen. The central government is providing the following avenues for resettlement/ re-employment of ex-servicemen:

a) Training programmes to re-orient retiring defence personnel towards civil employment.
b) Reservation of posts for providing re-employment opportunities in government/semi-government/public sector organisations.
c) Schemes for self-employment.

TRAINING PROGRAMMES

Training for preparing both ex-servicemen and retiring service personnel for their resettlement in civil life is one of the major functions of the Directorate General of Resettlement. Emphasis has been on employment/self-employment oriented training programmes so that new resettlement avenues, both for officers and other ranks, are opened.

A number of new courses and job-oriented training programmes have been included in the training schedule. Training includes inputs on managerial science as well as technology and know-how required in the civil field. Constant endeavour is made to improve the quality of training to enhance the post-employment opportunities of defence personnel and to equip them with necessary qualifications and expertise commensurate with the skill and aptitude of each individual in the desired field of settlement in civil life.

OFFICERS TRAINING

393 officers have been trained in various disciplines, during the training year 1998-99. The resettlement training

programmes range from vocational courses of 3 months duration to degree/diploma courses in Business Administration, Personnel Management, Hotel Management and Tourism, Human Resource Training and Development and so on of one to three years duration.

JCOs/OR AND REQUIREMENTS TRAINING

These programmes included vocational courses like security management, Export/import management, marketing/sales management and tourism and travel agency management. In an endeavour to further increase their employment potential, courses like computer hardware maintenance, diploma in medical laboratory and X-Ray/ECG technology, ceramic handicrafts, electroplating, machinist and lens making, computer science and applications, office automation, Computer-Aided Designing (CAD), printing technology and Desk Top Publishing (DTP), bee-keeping, poultry farming, crop production, dairy and animal husbandry, assistant security officer, industrial security and fire fighting courses and so on are being conducted.

The Directorate General Resettlement (DGR) has been conducting more than 400 courses for vocational training, besides courses at more than 200 ITIs for pre-and-post release training and On-the-Job-Training (OJT) courses at 85 PSUs/departmental undertakings as well as ex-servicemen resettlement training schemes.

RE-EMPLOYMENT

The central and state governments provide a number of concessions to ex-servicemen for their re-employment in central/state government posts. These include reservation of posts/ relaxation in age and educational qualifications, exemption from payment of application/examination fees, priority employment to disabled ex-servicemen and dependants of deceased service personnel on compassionate grounds.

RESERVATION FOR EX-SERVICEMEN IN GOVERNMENT JOBS

The central government has reserved ten per cent of Group 'C' posts and 20 per cent of Group 'D' posts for ex-servicemen. Central public sector undertakings and nationalised banks provide 14.5 per cent reservation in Group 'C' and 24.5 per cent in Group 'D' posts to ex-servicemen. 10 per cent posts of Assistant Commandants in paramilitary forces are also reserved for ex-servicemen.

In addition, most of the state governments, except the states of UP, Bihar, J&K, Kerala and Meghalaya, are providing reservations to ex-servicemen in the state government jobs. It has, however, not been possible to have statutory backing to the reservations being provided to ex-servicemen because of the overall ceiling of 50 per cent imposed by the supreme court and as 49.5 per cent reservation has already been provided in government jobs for SC/ST/OBC.

The reservation being provided to ex-servicemen is not of vertical nature as is the case of reservation for SC/ST/OBC but it is of horizontal nature, which implies that ex-servicemen selected against the vacancies reserved for them are subsequently adjusted against the relevant category *i.e.*, SC, ST, OBC or general to which they belong. There is also no carry forward of unfilled reserved vacancies under horizontal vacancies. Besides, with the shrinking of job opportunities in civil employment, large scale unemployment in the country and ever increasing competition, difficulties are faced in providing re-employment to ex-servicemen.

RELAXATION IN AGE

Ex-servicemen have been provided age relaxation to the extent of military service plus three years, against reserved/ unreserved vacancies in Group 'C' and 'D' posts and also in Group 'A' & 'B' posts, which are filled otherwise than by way of competitive examinations. The age relaxation is restricted to 5 years in Group 'A' & 'B' posts which are filled by competitive examinations.

RELAXATION IN EDUCATIONAL QUALIFICATION

Ex-servicemen are being granted relaxation in prescribed educational qualification. Army class I, II and III certificates have been equated to 8th, 6th and 4th class respectively in the civil. For reserved vacancies for which the minimum educational qualification is matriculation, an ex-servicemen who has put in at least 15 years of service and has passed army class I certificate or equivalent is considered eligible.

For the reserved jobs for which the minimum educational qualification is graduation, an ex-servicemen who has put in at least 15 years of service in the army and has passed matriculation or equivalent examination is considered eligible.

SECURITY AGENCIES

The Directorate General of Resettlement registers/sponsors security agencies for providing security guards to various public sector undertakings and industries in the private sector. The scheme offers self-employment opportunities to retired defence officers and employment opportunity to ex-PBOR. The Department of Public Enterprises (DPE) had issued instructions toll the PSUs to get security personnel through DGR-sponsored security agencies. The scheme had shown good results.

However, in December 1997, the said instructions were unilaterally withdrawn by the DPE. The matter was taken up with the Ministry of Industry, who have revived the scheme with effect from February 1, 1999. Instructions have been issued to all the Departments of Government of India to implement the scheme for PSUs under them.

PLACEMENT OF JCOS/OR

The number of ex-servicemen provided employment through the Directorate General Resettlement and Zila Sainik Welfare Officers in the states during the last five years are as follows:

Placement of JCOS/OR

	1994	1995	1996	1997	1998 (Jan.to June)
Central Government	4977	5080	5385	4023	2224
State Government	5678	4962	4076	4815	1085
Private Sector	5802	5628	4390	5424	1962
Security Agencies	3494	6150	8821	8873	2805
Total	19951	21820	22672	23135	8076

OFFICERS EMPLOYMENT

A total number of 319 officers were registered with the DGR, during the year 1998 (until October 1998). Officers' names were sponsored for employment for 307 posts during the same period. There has been a significant drop in fresh registration cases due to enhancement of the retirement age since May 1998.

SCHEMES FOR SELF-EMPLOYMENT

As it is not feasible to provide government jobs to all ex-Servicemen after their retirement from the armed forces, government has formulated several schemes for encouraging and giving financial support by way of loans to ex-Servicemen entrepreneurs intending to set up small and medium industries.

Important self-employment schemes are SEMFEX-I, SEMFEX-II and SEMFEX-III. Applications for sanction of loans are submitted by ex-servicemen directly to the concerned Zila Sainik Boards in the states.

The applications are scrutinised and those who satisfy eligibility criteria and other terms and conditions are recommended for sanction of loan through State Financial Corporations aided by Small Industries Development Bank of India (SIDBI), Scheduled Commercial Banks, District Central Cooperative Banks, State Land Development Banks and Regional Rural Banks aided by National Bank for Agriculture and Rural Development (NABARD).

Yearwise breakup of number of cases cleared for setting up production units in various schemes, loan amount sanctioned and actual disbursal of loan

Scheme	1994 -95	1995 -96	1996 -97	1997 -98
SEMFEX-I				
i) Number of cases	134.00	31.00	10.00	12.00
ii) Amount sanctioned	97.20	25.60	13.75	5.50
iii) Disbursal	75.45	24.12	10.41	5.50

SEMFEX- II				
i) Number of cases	538	571	415	359
ii) Amount sanctioned	325.44	448.97	289.16	179.76
iii)Disbursal	264.49	355.79	192.87	171.04
SEMFEX- III				
i) Number of cases	182.00	66.00	39.00	45.00
ii) Amount sanctioned	81.44	52.37	119.39	57.13
iii)Disbursal	66.09	32.94	105.47	48.84

EX-SERVICEMEN COAL TRANSPORT COMPANIES

Special provision exists for sponsoring ex-servicemen coal transport companies for the execution of work in the coal subsidiaries of Coal India Limited. The unemployed retired officers and JCOs registered with DGR are selected to form ex-servicemen coal transport companies and are sponsored to respective coal subsidiaries for five years, extendable by another two years. Totally 114 companies of ex-servicemen employing over 6,000 personnel are operating in six different coal subsidiaries of Coal India Limited.

ALLOTMENT OF OIL PRODUCT AGENCIES TO EX-SERVICEMEN

The Ministry of Petroleum and Natural Gas has reserved 8 per cent of the Oil Product Agencies *i.e.*, LPG, petrol pumps, kerosene and so on for disabled soldiers with disability of 50 per cent and above attributable to military service and widows and dependants of those who died in war/peace due to causes attributable to military service. The DGR sponsors eligible candidates for selection by the Oil Selection Board constituted by the Ministry of Petroleum & Natural Gas. Final allotment is made by their concerned oil company. Approximately 70-80 certificates are issued every year.

ALLOTMENT OF ARMY SURPLUS CLASS VB VEHICLES

Ex-servicemen and serving personnel due to retire within six months, can apply for Army Surplus Class V-B vehicles. The allotment is made by the army headquarters through nine vehicles depots. On an average, 2,000 applications are registered every year under this scheme.

RESERVATION OF CSD & LOW TECHNOLOGY ITEMS MANUFACTURED BY THE EX-SERVICEMEN ENTREPRENEURS

The Canteen Stores Department of India (CSDI) has reserved 15 per cent of the 30 selected CSD items and the Ministry of Defence has reserved 10 per cent of the 262 selected items, manufactured by ex-servicemen entrepreneurs under the Defence Purchase Programme.

GRANT OF PRICE SUBSIDY TO THE EX-SERVICEMEN'S SMALL SCALE INDUSTRIAL UNITS

Ex-servicemen manufacturing units supplying stores to defence establishments under Defence Purchase Programme are eligible for ten per cent price subsidy of the total value of stores supplied or Rs. 50,000/ whichever is less, in a financial year for five consecutive years. Totally 39 ex-servicemen units have been granted over Rs. 60 lakhs under the scheme so far.

ALLOTMENT OF PARKING SITES IN NEW DELHI

The New Delhi Municipal Committee currently has 105 parking lots in the area under its jurisdiction. Of these parking lots 50 per cent are reserved for ex-servicemen which are allotted to them on the basis of open limited tenders.

ALLOTMENT OF TYPEWRITERS/DUPLICATORS

Ex-servicemen are eligible to apply for a maximum of 5 repairable typewriters and one duplicator through DGR. These typewriters and duplicators are allotted by the Directorate of Military Records & Forms through Regional Stationery Depots on nominal payment. An average of 60 applicants are allotted these machines every year which includes officers and JCOs. As per feedback, these are used for setting up typewriting institutions in rural areas.

ALLOTMENT OF MOTHER DIARY/DMS MILK BOOTHS AND FRUIT & VEGETABLE OUTLETS

This scheme was launched in consultation with the National

Dairy Development Board (NDDB) to provide readymade booths with deep freezers, electronic weighing machines and other accessories costing approximately Rs. 8 lakh borne by NDDB. Ex-servicemen up to the rank of JCO or its equivalent, below the age 55 years are eligible for allotment of Mother Dairy milk booths and fruit & vegetable outlets till such a time as they attain 60 years of age.

More than 4500 ex-servicemen have benefited under the scheme since 1987 on a rotational basis. Based on the success of this scheme, other states have also been approached to provide similar facilities to ex-servicemen. Tamil Nadu and Karnataka have already responded with 50 per cent and 100 per cent reservation for allotment of automatic milk vending booths in their states. The Rajasthan government is also considering giving preferential treatment to ex-servicemen for allotment of milk vending booths.

WELFARE

The Kendriya Sainik Board (KSB) under the chairmanship of the Defence Minister has been established for laying down the general policy of the welfare of ex-servicemen and their dependants; for the administration of welfare funds and also for coordinating the work of the Rajya Sainik Boards (RSBs) and Zila Sainik Boards (ZSBs). The expenditure on the resettlement work in the states is shared by the central and the state governments in the ratio of 50:50. The KSB also administers the Armed Forces Flag Day Fund collected on Flag Day through sale of car flags and token flags. Various welfare activities are financed from the interest earning of the fund.

Financial assistance is provided to institutions such as Paraplegic Homes at Kirkee and Mohali, the Red Cross Society, Cheshire Homes, Military Hospitals, St. Dustan's After Care Organisation and the homes for taking care of old and physically handicapped ex-servicemen and their dependants.

FINANCIAL ASSISTANCE FROM DEFENCE MINISTER'S DISCRETIONARY FUND (RMDF)

A portion of the earnings of Armed Forces Flag Day Fund is

set apart as Raksha Mantri's Discretionary Fund and is used to provide financial assistance to poor and needy ex-servicemen who are in penury. This is given for various purposes, *viz*., medical treatment, marriage of daughters, repair of houses, education of children. Monthly financial assistance up to a period of two years is also provided to old and infirm ex-servicemen/widow of ex-servicemen living in penury.

CONCESSIONS AND FACILITIES

Undermentioned concessions and facilities are available to eligible personnel:

a) Free educational facilities to children of defence personnel killed or disabled in action.

b) Twenty five seats in the MBBS, one seat in BDS and two seats in engineering stream are available through KSB to dependants/wards of certain categories of defence personnel.

c) 25 per cent seats are reserved for the wards of serving and ex-servicemen personnel in Sainik Schools.

d) States/UTs have made reservation of seats in professional colleges/ITIs/ polytechnics for wards of serving and retired defence personnel.

e) Two educational grants of Rs. 600/- and Rs. 300/- p.m. per student is provided to wards of war bereaved, disabled, attributable and non-attributable peace time casualties respectively, housed in 35 war memorial hostels to enable them to pursue their studies.

f) Medical facilities

   i) Ex-servicemen, their families and families of deceased service personnel drawing pension of any kind are entitled to free outpatient treatment at military hospitals. These personnel can also be provided inpatient treatment in military hospitals subject to certain conditions. In addition to the existing military hospitals, 24 MI Rooms and 12 dental centres have been specially created from the funds provided by the services and KSB for providing medical facilities to ex-servicemen pensioners and their dependants.

ii) Ex-servicemen suffering from serious diseases are given financial assistance of up to 60 per cent of the total expenditure for treatment in civil hospitals in case they cannot raise funds from other sources. These are bypass surgery, open heart surgery/valve replacement, pacemaker implant, angiography/ angioplast, kidney/renal transplantation, dialysis, cancer and spastic paraplegics.

iii) Leading hospitals throughout the country have been empanelled from where the ex-servicemen can get treatment for serious diseases on payment of 40 per cent of the total expenditure. The remaining 60 per cent is paid directly to the hospitals by the KSB. For this purpose, the ex-Servicemen is required to submit a letter issued by KSB, to the hospital.

iv) Ex-servicemen not availing medical facilities from military hospitals can choose to draw Rs. 100/- every month for medical purposes.

g) *Travel concessions*: Following concessions are available to war widows/ gallantry award winners, which can be availed on production of identity card issued by KSB:

i) *Rail travel concession*: 75 per cent concessions in rail fare for travel in II Class is available to war widows, including those of IPKF casualties. Besides, recipients and widows of posthumous recipients of Chakra series of gallantry awards are entitled or free rail pass for travelling in Class I/II AC Sleeper.

ii) *Travel concession*: Certain categories of personnel are eligible to 50 per cent concession in fare for air travel in domestic flights of the Indian Airlines.

h) *Reservation of house-sites/houses*: A majority of states have made reservations for serving/retired Armed Forces personnel in allotment of house sites/ houses.

i) *Grant for repair of houses*: Financial assistance is provided especially to war widows/war disabled for repair of houses on 50 per cent cost sharing basis with state governments up to an extent of Rs. 10,000/-.

j) *Sainik rest house facilities*: Over 252 Sainik Rest Houses have been created in the country which provide transit facilities to ex-servicemen and their dependants at nominal rates.

k) *Cash award/annuity/cash in lieu of land for gallantry/ non-gallantry award winners*: The states/UTs provide cash award/annuity/cash in lieu of land for gallantry/ nongallantry award winners.

ACHIEVEMENTS 1998-99

Major welfare measures/achievements made by the KSB during 1998-99 are mentioned below:

a) Based on the recommendations of the Ministry of Defence during the recent past, a few states, *i.e.*, Goa. Kerala, Mizoram, NCT of Delhi and UT of Chandigarh have enhanced the rates of monthly financial assistance to Rs. 300/- or more for their World War-II veterans/ widows.

b) The Assam government has decided to provide Rs. 2 lakh to next of kin (NOK) of defence personnel belonging to Assam, killed in counter-insurgency operations in the state. The government of Tripura has also enhanced rates of ex-gratia payment from Rs. 25,000/- to Rs. 50,000/- for the defence personnel who are killed in extremist violence while on duty in the state.

c) During the year, a record amount of Rs. 22.56 lakhs has been sanctioned as financial assistance to 248 ex-servicemen/dependants in penury, from the Defence Minister's Discretionary Fund. During this period, 202 ex-servicemen/dependants have been provided financial assistance of Rs. 85 lakhs for treatment of serious diseases from Armed Forces Flag Day Fund.

d) Government orders on the recommendations of the Fifth Pay Commission on pensionary benefits to ex-servicemen, have been forwarded to all the Rajya Sainik Boards for further dissemination to the Zila Sainik Boards under their jurisdiction for information.

PENSION TO ARMED FORCES PERSONNEL

Armed forces are required to maintain a youthful profile at

all times for the maintenance and upkeep of the highest degree of combat efficiency. Service personnel are retired/ released at a younger age as compared to civilian employees. Approximately 50,000 service personnel retire every year.

In recognition of their difficult service conditions, early retirement and the supreme sacrifice of life in the interest of the nation, armed forces personnel are granted pensionary benefits at somewhat liberal scale as compared to their civilian counterparts. The nature of retirement/release from service determines the admissibility of the type of pension in the cases of armed forces personnel.

RETIRING/SERVICE PENSION

Commissioned officers of the army, navy and air force after rendering the prescribed 20 years of minimum qualifying service and the Personnel Below Officer Rank (PBORs) after completion of 15 years of service (20 years in the case NCSE), become eligible to retiring/service pension. Retiring/service pension is calculated at 50 per cent of the average reckonable emoluments as in the case of civil pensioners. In view of their early retirement the benefit of added years of service is given to the armed forces personnel while calculating their qualifying service for pension.

This benefit ranges from nine years for Captains and below to three years for Generals and five years in the case personnel below officer's rank. While in the case of officers, pension is calculated on the basis of the average pay drawn during the last ten months of service, in the case of PBORs, it is calculated with reference to the maximum pay of the rank held for ten months preceding retirement. For calculating gratuity, a uniform weightage of five years added service is given to all ranks.

DISABILITY PENSION

Disability pension is granted to an armed forces personnel who is disabled during service and is boarded out on account of a disease/injury/wound attributable to or aggravated by military service provided that the disability assessed by the Medical Board is 20 per cent or more. Disability pension is granted in addition to service pension and/or gratuity as admissible depending on the length of service. Disability pension consists of service element and disability element. The amount of service element is equal to the normal retiring/service pension.

The service element subject to a minimum of Rs. 1,275/- is also payable when the length of service rendered is less than the minimum pensionable service. Personnel with 100 per cent disability are also paid a Constant Attendance Allowance on the recommendations of the Medical Board. In all other cases, where the personnel are invalidated out of service with a disability neither attributable to nor aggravated by military service, invalid pension is granted, if the service rendered is ten years or more. If the service is less than ten years, invalidating gratuity depending upon the length of service is paid.

The 5th Central Pay Commission has made recommendations inter alia for enhancement of the minimum disability element of disability pension from Rs. 375/- per month to Rs. 1350/- per month. Final decisions with regard to the various recommendations relating to disability pension are yet to be taken by the government and the same will be suitably notified in due course.

WAR INJURY PENSION

In case of 100 per cent disability in war or warlike operations, the pay last drawn at the time of invalidment is paid to the service personnel as war injury pension on monthly basis. The amount of war injury pension in case of invalidment is proportionately reduced where the degree of disability is less, subject to a minimum of 60 per cent of the last pay drawn in the case of commissioned officers and 80 per cent of the last pay drawn in the PBORs.

War injury pension at this rate is also paid in cases where the disability is less than 20 per cent on invalidment. Armed forces personnel who are retained in service despite war injury and retired subsequently are given an option either to draw lumpsum compensation in lieu of war injury element or to draw war injury pension at the time of subsequent retirement foregoing lumpsum compensation. The 5th Central Pay Commission's recommendations relating to grant of war injury pension are at present under consideration of the government.

FAMILY PENSION

Ordinary family pension: Families of armed forces personnel who die during service or after retirement with pension, are granted ordinary family pension at uniform rate of 30 per cent of the reckonable emoluments. The amount of minimum family pension which earlier was Rs. 375/- per month has been raised to Rs. 1275/- per month with effect from January 1, 1996 on the basis of the recommendations of the 5th Central Pay Commission. If the deceased personnel had rendered seven years or more service, then the family is given family pension at double the rate of the first seven years or up to the time when deceased would have reached the age of 65 years, whichever is earlier. The amount of enhanced family pension will, however, not be more than 50 per cent of the emoluments, or the retiring pension if the death takes place after retirement but before 65 years of age.

Special family pension: If a service personnel dies on account of causes attributable to or aggravated by military service, the widow with children is granted special family pension at the rate of 60 per cent of the reckonable emoluments drawn by the deceased, subject to a minimum of Rs. 750/- and a maximum of Rs. 2500/ (pre-revised). The 5th Central Pay Commission's recommendations for grant of Special Family Pension in such cases at the rate of 60 per cent of reckonable emoluments without ceiling, are under consideration of the government and appropriate orders would be issued as soon as the decisions in this regard are taken.

Liberalised special family pension: In recognition of sacrifice of life in war or warlike operations/counter-insurgency operations/ action against terrorists/ extremists *etc.*, the families of the deceased armed forces personnel are granted Liberalised Special Family Pension equal to the pay last drawn by the deceased. Dearness relief as revised from time to time is also paid along with the pension.

In addition to the grant of Special Family Pension/ Liberalised Special Family Pension, orders have also been issued by the Ministry of Defence, effective from August 1, 1997, in pursuance of the recommendations of the 5th Central Pay Commission for payment of ex-gratia amount to the family of a service personnel in the event of his death during the course of performance of bonafide official duty as given below:

a) Death occurring due to accidents in the course of performance of duties—Rs. 5.00 lakh.

b) Death occurring in the course of performance of duties attributable to acts of violence by terrorists, antisocial elements, and so on—Rs. 5.00 lakh.

c) Death occurring during (i) enemy action in international war or border skirmishes and (ii) action against militants, terrorists, extremists, and so on—Rs. 7.50 lakh.

IMPLEMENTATION OF 5TH CENTRAL PAY COMMISSION'S RECOMMENDATIONS

Decisions on other recommendations of the 5th Central Pay Commission relating to enhancement/revision of the rates of disability pension/special family pension/war injury pension and *etc.,* are yet to be taken by the nodal department of the central government *i.e.*, the department of Pensions and Pensioners' Welfare. Necessary orders in this regard would be issued when the same become available. In pursuance of the decisions taken by the government on the recommendations of the 5th Central Pay Commission, orders have been issued by the Ministry of Defence for revision of pension with effect from January 1, 1996 of pre-January 1, 1986/ pre- and post January 1, 1996 defence pensioners/ family pensioners.

The important features of these orders, inter alia, include grant of minimum retiring pension/family pension at Rs. 1275/ per month, enhancement of the maximum limit of service/death gratuity from Rs. 2.5 lakh to Rs. 3.5 lakh and payment of a medical allowance at the rate of Rs. 100/- per month to all armed forces pensioners who are not provided medical facilities as outdoor patients in armed forces hospitals/MI rooms.

EXPENDITURE DEFENCE PENSIONS

Number of defence pensioners at present is estimated to be about 17 lakh. Pension is disbursed through 25,000 branches of public sector banks, 540 treasuries, 60 defence pension disbursing offices and 4 pay and accounts offices scattered all over India. The annual expenditure on defence pensions during the last five years has been as follows:

Year	Pension Disbursed (Rs. in crore)
1994-95	2704.10
1995-96	3197.12
1996-97	3683.00
1997-98	4947.42
1998-99 (B.E.)	5923.58

13

Armed Forces and Civil Authorities

The armed forces render assistance to civil authorities, when called upon to do so, for the maintenance of law and order, essential services, and for organising relief and rescue operations during natural calamities. To ensure a timely response, the armed forces maintain regular liaison with the civil authorities, and meetings are held at different levels with civilians officials to coordinate various facets of aid.

Maintenance of Law and Order and Anti-militant Operations

The army's active assistance to the state governments of the north-east in counter-insurgency/anti militancy operations has helped them to contain the insurgency. In Assam, sustained military operations under the aegis of revitalised unified headquarters, resulted in effective neutralisation of militants besides keeping them holed up in 'trans-border safe sanctuaries'. Consequently, during 1998 insurgency in the state remained at low ebb.

However, in a bid to show to the masses that their writ still runs in the state, militant outfits, specially the United Liberation Front of Assam (ULFA), continued to engage soft targets/indulge in sabotage activity. The Bodos on the other hand focused their attention on the Bodo Autonomous Council issue and to draw attention of the centre/state governments towards their demands, resorted to sabotage and other depredatory activities including ethnic cleansing in areas of the Bodo Autonomous Council.

In Nagaland the ceasefire with the National Socialist Council of Nagaland (ISAK-Muvah) [NSCN(IM)] and other groups has been monitored/enforced virtually single-handed by the army since August 1997. While the ceasefire has been holding out with NSCN(IM) and other groups, the National Socialist Council of Nagaland (Khaplang) [NSCN (K)] remained recalcitrant.

The army, therefore, was compelled to recommence operations against the outfit. However, in view of overtures by tribal organisations, the operations against the group were suspended for a period of two months from November 15, 1998. Involvement of all groups in the peace initiative will facilitate finding a lasting solution to the Nagaland problem.

In Jammu & Kashmir local support for militancy declined progressively as the local population had seen through the designs of the sponsors of terrorism. A desperate effort is being made by the external sponsors to sustain the proxy war by infiltrating more foreign mercenaries specially trained in assembling and planting sophisticated Improvised Explosive Devices (IEDs) for standoff attacks against soft targets/VIPs. An estimated 700-800 foreign mercenaries are operating in the state.

Measures such as synergisation of operations of all security forces, improved intelligence and redeployment of forces resulted in the elimination of 793, apprehension of 468 and surrender of 104 militants, while recovering a total of over 1606 weapons during the year. Relentless operations continue throughout the winter to eliminate the mercenaries who had infiltrated into the state. The army's assistance was requisitioned by the government of Tamil Nadu following a series of bomb blasts that had rocked Coimbatore town on the eve of a proposed political rally.

Assistance during Natural Calamities

During the period under review, the army's assistance was sought by various state governments, for relief and rescue operations at a number of flood affected areas in the country. Army personnel evacuated thousands of marooned people besides assisting the civil administration in medical and material relief. Of significance, were the relief/rescue operations in the following states/areas:

(a) *Floods in Uttar Pradesh and Bihar*: Eastern Uttar Pradesh (UP) and Champaran districts of Bihar were virtually cut off from the rest of the country owing to heavy floods, causing serious losses to both life and property. A total of 28 columns, along with medical teams, were provided by the army from July to September 1998, to restore normalcy. The army's assistance was rendered in terms of evacuation of marooned civilians, provision of medical aid and large-scale distribution of food packets/relief material, both by land and air.

(b) *Malpa tragedy (Kumaon Hills, UP)*: Braving tough and inclement weather, approximately one thousand army men provided immediate assistance in rescue and safe transportation of survivors, besides retrieval of dead bodies from the debris. Other facets of the aid rendered by the Army included provisioning of communications, track construction, distribution of rations/essential supplies, medical aid and air effort by the army aviation helicopters.

(c) *Cyclone in Gujarat*: Apropos cyclonic storms that engulfed coastal Gujarat and the Rann of Kutch during June 1998, the army had provided five relief columns along with specialist equipment and medical teams.

MAINTENANCE OF ESSENTIAL SERVICES ARMY

Army assisted the civil administration in maintenance of essential services in the following disciplines:

a) Provision of army nursing staff to various government hospitals in the union territory of Delhi during May 1998, following a strike by nurses in the capital.

b) Provision of five technical columns to the Uttar Pradesh government in July 1998, following a strike by the Uttar Pradesh State Electricity Board (UPSEB) staff.

OTHER TYPE OF ASSISTANCE

Antarctica expedition: The army logistic support contingent comprising two officers, two JCOs and nine other ranks was provided to the Department of Ocean Development, the Government of India for the 17th and 18th Antarctica Expeditions. Tasks undertaken by the contingent are construction, repair and maintenance of permanent stations; running of life-support systems and overland transportation of men and material on the continent.

Army teams have also been undertaking other humanitarian tasks, over and above their laid down charter. On June 1, 1998, army personnel, despite difficult weather/ terrain conditions, rescued four survivors from a Russian helicopter that had crashed on the continent.

Restoring national highway-22: Consequent to the flash floods resulting in the severe disruption of NH-22 during September 1997, the Army assistance in the form of seven bridges were provided to the state government of Himachal Pradesh to restore vital communication link.

Restoration of water supply in North West Delhi: To ensure continuous water supply to the residents of north-west Delhi, the army launched a bridge at Hyderpur during July/ August 1998 to provide support to the water pipes that had sagged due to a breach in the embankment of the canal.

NAVY

Cyclone relief operations—Port Kandla and Jamnagar: The severe cyclonic storm, which hit the coast of Gujarat just north of Porbandar on June 9, 1998, left a trail of havoc with a large number of lives lost both at sea and ashore. The severity of the storm was the most at Kandla port. The Indian navy responded quickly by pressing in all available resources into undertaking relief operation in a swift and efficient manner to provide succour to the affected. The navy also undertook efforts to restore communication links and essential services as also the port operations in a record time thus saving vital earnings to the exchequer.

Flood relief operations: Heavy rains in the northern Gangetic plains resulted in unprecedented floods in vast areas of Bihar and West Bengal. The magnitude of the calamity was of alarming proportion. The navy mobilised immediate relief operations by providing medical and diving relief operations through 29 naval doctors, 50 medical personnel, 25 divers and 19 personnel from different trades. Relief operations spanned from September 15 to October 9, 1998 and spread over Malda district in West Bengal and Samastipur in Bihar covering the village of Hasanpur, Kaliachak, Mahananda Tola, Bhilaimar Delta and Panchanandpura and areas in and around Malda itself.

Similar relief operations were undertaken in many districts along the Godavari river following heavy rains in Andhra Pradesh. Naval relief teams were despatched to areas near Vijaywada to provide relief in villages which were cut off and had no means of communications.

Other relief operations: During the year, naval divers provided assistance to various state governments and District Administrations for rescue of personnel and recovering of bodies in various accidents *viz.,* operations in Wardha river to rescue coal miners at Ambernath, to rescue passengers of Konark Express in October 1998, and so on. Responding to a call for medical assistance from a merchant vessel *Pearl* of Abu Dhabi on October 21/22, 1998, a mother and her prematurely born baby were airlifted by naval units and safely brought ashore. Assistance rendered by the navy highlights its commitment towards nation building in addition to its primary role in war.

INDIAN AIR FORCE (IAF)

Flood relief: The Indian Air Force has rendered yeoman service in aid to civil power. Extensive flood and cyclone relief operations were carried out by the Indian Air Force during the year. Numerous sorties were carried out airdropping tons of relief load as well as rescuing stranded people in the affected areas of Gujarat, Bihar, Rajasthan, Uttar Pradesh, Arunachal Pradesh, Assam and West Bengal. Indian Air Force helicopters were also pressed into service towards emergency requests by the governments of Jammu and Kashmir and Uttar Pradesh to assist in dealing with massive landslides and floods.

Malpa tragedy: There was a massive landslide at Malpa village in the Uttar Pradesh hills during August 1998. The 12th batch of Kailash Mansarovar Yatris camping at Malpa village were swept away and buried under the landslides caused by the torrential rains. This resulted in the loss of approximately 120 lives.

The Indian Air Force swung into action to provide immediate relief to stranded pilgrims conveying the survivors to safety and carrying the bodies of the deceased to Dharchula and Pithoragarh.

Disaster relief: The IAF has been extensively involved in disaster relief particularly during the latter half of 1998. For flood relief and natural calamities, over 900 sorties were launched in 1998, representing an eighteen-fold increase over 1996. The figures for casualty evacuation and aid to civil power have shown dramatic increases over previous years as the air force strives to meet all tasks required of it.

14

National Cadet Corps (NCC)

The National Cadet Corps (NCC), established under the NCC Act, 1948, has completed 50 years of its existence. The NCC strives to provide the youth of this country opportunities for all-round development with a sense of commitment, dedication, self-discipline and moral values, so that they become good leaders and useful citizens and can take their appropriate place in all walks of life in the service of the nation.

The progress and quality of training is reviewed and changes incorporated to bring about improvements. The total strength of NCC cadets is 11.68 lakh approximately. The wing-wise distribution of the enrolled cadet strength is as under:

a) Army Wing	:	8,02,273
b) Air Wing	:	58,947
c) Naval Wing	:	57,655
d) Girls Wing	:	1,24,753

The NCC's presence can be felt in almost all the districts of the country covering 6,625 schools and 4,244 colleges.

Training of NCC Officers

Various types of courses are conducted for the NCC officers and permanent instructional staff at the Officer Training School (OTS), Kamptee and the Women Officers Training School (WOTS), Gwalior.

TRAINING OF CADETS

Camp training

a) *Annual training camps*: 4,97,500 cadets attended 1,110 camps organised during 1998-99.

b) *Centrally organised camps*: 6,900 cadets attended the centrally organised camps conducted at various places during 1998-99.

c) *National Integration Camps (NIC)*: During the year, 56 camps had been planned in which 41,250 cadets participated, A special NIC was held at Port Blair from February 15-26, 1999 in which 64 cadets from the main land and 50 from the Andaman and Nicobar Islands participated.

d) *Nau sainik camps:* The Nau Sainik Camp was held on November 2-13, 1998 at Vishakhapatnam in which 400 Senior Division and 160 Senior Wing cadets participated. In addition, a Naval Technical Training Camp was conducted for the first time from May 25 to June 6, 1998 in two batches of 50 cadets each drawn from an engineering colleges. This will continue on an annual basis.

e) *Vayu sainik camp*: 841 Air Wing cadets participated in the Vayu Sainik Camp held in October 1998 for a period of 12 days.

f) *Attachment training*: NCC activities motivate the cadets to join the armed forces by providing them exposure to the Services way of life. 10,000 Army Wing Cadets, 120 Air Wing Cadets and 275 Naval Wing Cadets were attached with army, naval and air force units and stations during 1998-99. 64 Senior Division Cadets were attached to the Indian Military Academy, Dehradun and 16 Senior Wing Cadets with the Officers Training Academy, Chennai, for a period of 2 weeks. 1,000 girl cadets were attached with various military hospitals during the year.

g) *Gliding and flying*: NCC Air Wing Cadets are exposed to gliding and flying as part of their training. Gliding facilities are provided at 34 Air Squadrons and power flying is done on Pushpak, Cessna aircraft at 13 selected flying clubs.

h) *Foreign cruise*: Every year, a foreign cruise is organised for the NCC cadets on boats and ships of the first training squadron of the navy. Five NCC cadets proceeded to Mauritius and Seychelles on September 19, 1998.

i) *Shooting*: Thirty two NCC cadets participated in the VIII All India G.V. Mavlankar Shooting Championship at Asansole, West Bengal from December 28, 1998 to January 3, 1999 and at the XXXXI NRAI Shooting Championship.

Adventure training

Mountaineering: NCC has conducted 42 mountaineering expeditions since 1970. This year, the Senior Division boy cadets successfully climbed Hanuman Tiba Peak at a height of 19,760 feet and the Senior Wing Girl Cadets climbed Ladakhi peak at a height of 17,526 feet. Basic and advanced mountaineering courses are conducted for cadets at Himalayan Mountaineering Institute (HMI), Darjeeling, Nehru Mountaineering Institute (NMI), Uttarkashi and Mountaineering and Allied Sports (MAS), Manali.

Trekking expeditions: Ten trekking expeditions for cadets from different parts of the country are conducted every year. All ten have been completed successfully in 1998-99.

Cycle and motorcycle expedition: Five cycle and motorcycle expeditions at the national and state level have been completed this year.

Para jumping: Every year, 20 boys and 20 girl NCC Cadets are trained at the Para Training School, Agra. In 1998-99, the para jumping course was conducted during November 2- 22, 1998.

Slithering: Ten Senior Division and Senior Wing Cadets were trained in slithering to participate and demonstrate during the NCC's Prime Minister's Rally on January 27, 1999.

Sailing, wind surfing and kayaking: Each NCC State Directorate planned at least one sailing expedition competing for the Republic Day Banner. A sailing regetta was held at *INS Chilka* during January 11- 20, 1999.

Sports and games: The second NCC games were held during August 2-15, 1998 at New Delhi. Totally 1,350 cadets from all over the country participated in the NCC games including volleyball, football, athletics, unarmed combat and presentation of murals and patriotic pageants.

The Sports Authority of India selected 21 probables from cadets who participated in the NCC games 1998.

Youth exchange programme: The NCC has an ongoing youth exchange programme with Singapore, Bangladesh, Sri Lanka and Nepal.

It is proposed to convert the existing non-reciprocal programmes into reciprocal ones and enhance the programme with SAARC countries.

Community development: NCC cadets participate in a number of community development programmes covering adult education, tree plantation, environment awareness, slum clearance, assistance during natural calamities, social service and health related activities.

International award for unemployed in India (Duke of Edinburgh Award): More than 7,000 NCC cadets earned the Duke of Edinburgh Award in 1998-99.

CENTRAL ADVISORY COMMITTEE (CAC) FOR THE NCC

A statutory Central Advisory Committee (CAC) has been appointed to advise the government on policy matters connected with the administration and constitution of the NCC.

The 39th Meeting of the Central Advisory Committee was held on September 30, 1998 under the chairmanship of the Defence Minister. The Committee reviewed the progress of followup action on the decisions taken at the last meeting and took the following decisions:

i) The Ministry of Human Resource Development was requested to arrange and meet its financial obligations to facilitate proper functioning of NCC in the Kendriya Vidyalayas.

ii) The Defence Minister would address all the Chief Ministers for greater involvement of NCC cadets in community development activities.

iii) Directorate General NCC was advised to approach the army headquarters for release of equipment in the army and other services for support in equipment.

15

Academic Activities

The Ministry of Defence encourages and promotes both academic and adventure activities through autonomous institutions which are provided regular financial assistance. The institutions are:

i) The Institute for Defence Studies and Analyses, New Delhi

ii) Mountaineering Institutes at Darjeeling and Uttarkashi.

iii) The Jawahar Institute of Mountaineering and Winter Sports (JIM) at Aru, Kashmir.

Their important activities during the period are as follows:

Institute for Defence Studies and Analysis

The Institute for Defence Studies and Analyses (IDSA) was established in November 1965 to initiate studies and research on problems of national security and the impact of defence measures on economic, political and social developments.

Over the years, the institute has evolved as a premier research institution carrying out policy-related authoritative studies on national and international security issues. The institute is a registered body under the Registration of Societies Act III of 1860 as amended from time to time, and is governed by an Executive Council elected by the members of the institute.

The institute is accessible to political leaders, scholars, media, civil and defence service officers, and others who have an interest in problems of national security. During 1998-99, the tempo of activities was maintained and strengthened in selected areas. Impetus was given to greater interaction and cooperation with other institutions and organisations dealing with security and strategic issues.

The Standing Committee on Defence of the Parliament continued to draw heavily upon the literature, information and expertise of the institute. Numerous institutions, including the defence establishments in India and abroad, continued to draw upon the experience and expertise of the institute to support their training, research and orientation programmes. Interaction with the defence services continued to flourish.

The Ministries of Defence and External Affairs continued to take active interest in supporting the activities of the institute. The institute continued to pursue its dedicated research projects on the geopolitics of energy, proliferation of small arms and its implications for national and international security and International Atomic Energy Association (IAEA) Safeguards System. The research projects US foreign policy towards India, India and the ASEAN, Central Asia, nuclear proliferation and disarmament, and so on, continued to progress according to plan.

The institute organised a major international conference in January 1999 on the theme of Asian Security in the 21st Century where eminent decision-makers and opinion shapers, including members of parliament, actively participated. The Institute continued to play host to visits and addresses by eminent dignitaries from India and abroad. It organised three national seminars/ conferences on "Financial Crisis in East Asia and its impact on International Security" and "Defence Spending and Expenditure Control". It organised regular fortnightly seminars on issues under study besides organising numerous round table discussions. The following international seminars were organised during the year:

i) International conference on "Asian Security in the 21st Century" in New Delhi, January 1999.

ii) Third India-Japan dialogue on political and security issues titled "Enhancing Peace and Cooperation in Asia" organised jointly with Japan Institute for International Affairs, Tokyo held in Tokyo, December 1998.

iii) Second Indo-Israeli Seminar organised, jointly with BESA, Tel-Aviv held in New Delhi, 1998.

iv) Joint India-Italy symposium on "Global Security in the Next 50 Years" held in New Delhi, 1998.

v) Second workshop on "Monitoring Technologies and Cooperative Monitoring" organised jointly with CMC, Sandia National Laboratories, New Mexico, USA, held in New Delhi, 1998.

During the year, research faculty of the Institute published the following books:

i) *Tools, of Terror: Light Weapons and India's Security*, by Ms. Tara Kartha, published by Knowledge World and IDSA, New Delhi, 1999.

ii) *Pakistan: A Withering State?* by Sreedhar and Nilesh Bhagat, published by Wordsmith, New Delhi, 1999.

iii) *Indo-US Relations into the 21st Century*, by Dr. Chintamani Mahapatra, published by Knowledge World and IDSA, New Delhi, 1998.

iv) *Nuclear India*, edited by Jasjit Singh, published by Knowledge World and IDSA, New Delhi, 1998.

v) *Cooperative Peace in Asia*, edited by Jasjit Singh, published by IDSA, New Delhi, 1998.

vi) *India's Armed Forces: Fifty Years of War and Peace*, authored by Maj Gen Ashok Krishna, published by Lancers International, New Delhi, 1998.

vii) *Afghan Turmoil—Changing Equations*, edited by T. Sreedhar Rao and Mahendra Ved, published by Himalaya Publishers, New Delhi, 1998.

viii) *Mutual security: The case of India-Nepal*, authored by Sangeeta Taphliyal, published by Lancers Publishers and Distributors, New Delhi, 1998.

In addition, the following monographs in the Delhi Papers series were also published by the faculty:

i) *Redefining Japanese Security* by Sanjana Joshi, Delhi Paper No.5, IDSA 1998.

ii) *The Afghan Conflict and India* by P. Stobdan, Delhi Paper No.6, IDSA 1998.

iii) *French Strategic Doctrine* by Tara Kartha, Delhi Paper No. 7, 1998.

iv) *India and ASEAN* by GVC Naidu, Delhi Paper No. 8, 1998.

The government has allotted 4.5 acres of land in Subroto Park area and approved Rs. 17 crore from the National Defence Fund in principle for a designed-to-requirement permanent building.

MOUNTAINEERING INSTITUTES

There are three mountaineering institutes, namely the Himalayan Mountaineering Institute (HMI), Darjeeling in West Bengal, the Nehru Institute of Mountaineering (NIM), Uttarkashi in Uttar Pradesh, and the Jawahar Institute of Mountaineering and Winter Sports (JIM), Aru with temporary headquarters at Batote (J&K). These institutes are run as private registered societies. The Defence Minister is the President of these institutes. The Chief Minister of the respective state is the Vice-President of the institute.

These institutes are governed by separate Executive Councils consisting of members elected by the general bodies, nominees from amongst donors and/or persons who are likely to promote the cause of the institute and representatives of central and state governments. A representative each of the Ministry of Defence and state government acts as Secretary of the institute.

The HMI, Darjeeling, was founded on November 14, 1954 by the then Prime Minister, Pandit Jawaharlal Nehru, to commemorate the first ascent of Mount Everest by the late Tenzing Norgay along with Sir Edmund Hillary on May 29,1953. With the establishment of this institute, an impetus to mountaineering as a sport was provided in India.

To give a further boost to mountaineering and to inculcate the spirit of adventure in youth, the NIM, Uttarkashi was set up in October 1965 and the JIM at Aru in J&K in October 1983. In view of the disturbances in the valley, students were reluctant to come to Aru for training.

Accordingly, it was decided to shift the institute temporarily to Batote on the Jammu side to Banihal with effect from August 10, 1990. The broad objectives of the mountaineering Institutes are:

a) To impart theoretical and practical training in mountaineering and rock climbing techniques;

b) To interest in and love for mountains and exploration; and

c) To encourage and provide training in winter sports.

The institutes conduct Basic and Advanced Mountaineering Courses, Method of Instruction Course (MOI), Search and Rescue Course and Adventure Courses. The syllabi, duration, age limit of participants and grading system for various types of course are uniform at all the institutes.

During the lean period, the institutes detail their instructors to conduct rock climbing courses at the request of mountaineering clubs/ organisations around the country. The instructors also join various expeditions. Trainees for these courses come from all parts of the country and include army, air force, navy, ITBP and BSF personnel, NCC cadets, university/college youth sponsored by the University Grants Commission and private students.

In the year up to December 1998, the institutes conducted the following courses:

Institute	Basic	Advanced	Adventure	MOI	S&R
HMI	5	2	5	1	-
NIM	5	3	6	-	1
JIM	2	-	-	-	-

The number of students imparted training in these courses is as under:

Institute (HMI/ NIM/ JIM)	Basic	Advanced	Adventure	MOI S&R
Men	593	119	361	10 33
Women 127	41	105	- 6	

Institutes at Darjeeling and Uttarkashi have separate stores of mountaineering equipment for loan to the Indian mountaineering expeditions on nominal hire charges. In order to extend promotion of adventure activities and to strengthen friendly ties between India and Argentina, it was proposed to organise two Joint HMI-Argentina Mountaineering Expeditions—one in Indian Himalayas and the other in Argentina to Mount Aconcagua.

Under this Institutional Cooperation Programme between HMI, Darjeeling and Federation Regional de Andinismo Escalada, Republic of Argentina, the first joint HMI-Argentina Mountaineering Expedition to Mountd Kamet & Abi Gamin was organised by Himalayan Mountaineering Institute, Darjeeling in the Garhwal Himalayas during August/September 1998.

The second joint expedition to Mount Aconcagua was conducted during February-March 1999. A seven member HMI team led by the Principal of the Institute left India for Argentina on February 6, 1999. As a part of celebrations of the 50th anniversary of India's Independence, the Himalayan Mountaineering Institute also conducted a SAARC Adventure Camp from April 16 to 26, 1998 with financial assistance from the Ministry of External Affairs. Twenty two participants including nationals from Pakistan, Nepal and India took part in the camp.

In the meeting of the Executive Council of the Institute held on November 6, 1997 under the Chairmanship of the Defence Minister and attended by Chief Minister, J&K, it was decided to shift the institute to Sonamarg area. The state government agreed to provide land and infrastructure. The Principal, JIM in coordination with the concerned officers of the government of J&K did a reconnaissance of the area for selection of suitable site for the location of the institute in Sonamarg area. However, no suitable site could be found for a permanent set up of the institute in Sonamarg as the area becomes inaccessible during winter. On an experimental basis, a basic mountaineering course was conducted in Sonamarg area from August 17 to September 11, 1998. Eigtheen students from the State participated in this course.

CERMONIALS, HONOURS AND AWARDS

The Ministry of Defence is responsible for organising national functions like the Republic Day Parade, the Beating Retreat Ceremony, the Independence Day Celebration and the Martyr's Day Function. Defence Investiture Ceremonies at the Rashtrapati Bhawan for presentation of Gallantry and Distinguished Service Awards are also organised by the Ministry of Defence in association with the President's Secretariat. The organisation of these ceremonies requires coordination of a large number of activities amongst various ministries/departments.

EX-GRATIA LUMPSUM COMPENSATION

Consequent upon the recommendation of the Vth Central Pay Commission, government orders on payment of ex-gratia lumpsum compensation were issued on September 22, 1998 for families of defence service personnel who die in the performance of their bona fide official duties. The following ex-gratia lumpsum compensation will be paid to the next of kin of the personnel:

a) Death occurring due to accidents in the course of performance of duties—Rs. 5.00 Lakh
b) Death occurring in the course of performance of duties attributable to acts of violence by terrorists, antisocial elements, and so on—Rs. 5.00 Lakh
c) Death occurring during enemy action in international war or border skirmishes; and action against militants, terrorists, extremists, and so on—Rs. 7.50 lakh.

The graded structure of ex-gratia lumpsum compensation takes into account the hardship and risks involved in certain assignments, the intensity and magnitude of the tragedy and deprivation to the families of breadwinner in different circumstances, the expectations of the employer from the employees to function in extreme circumstances, and so on. The compensation is intended to provide an additional insurance and security to employees who are required to function under trying circumstances and are exposed to different kinds of risks in the performance of their duties.

REDRESSAL OF PUBLIC GRIEVANCES

Public grievance petitions received through the Department of Administrative Reforms and Public Grievances and directly from the petitioners as well as complaint boxes named as 'Raksha Mantri's Complaint Box' that have been installed at the reception of various buildings where offices of the Ministry of Defence are located, are reviewed at the level of Defence Secretary on a fortnightly basis. A quarterly meeting is also held under the chairmanship of Defence Secretary to review the pending cases of public grievances.

OFFICIAL LANGUAGE DIVISION (OL)

The official Language Division is responsible for implementation of the official language policy of the union in the Ministry of Defence and its various organisations including the three services headquarters, Inter-service organisations, defence undertakings, ordnance factories, and so on. The division comprises one Director (OL), one Deputy Director (OL), four O.L. Sections with one Assistant Director (OL) each and the required number of translators and other staff.

The division remained engaged in the task of spreading and propagating Hindi in the above-mentioned offices as per provisions of the Official Language Act, rules and orders/ instructions issued by the Department of Official Language, Ministry of Home Affairs, during the year under report. Concerted efforts aimed at increasing the use of Hindi at all levels in the ministry ranging from sections to highest ranking officers were made during the year and several measures were taken for this purpose which include provision of bilingual facility on modern electronic equipments like electronic typewriters, computers, and so on.

ORIGINAL ARRANGEMENT OF TRANSLATION IN HINDI

Apart from ensuring the cent per cent compliance of the provisions contained in Section 3(3) of the Official Language Act and Rule 5 of the Official Language Rules, emphasis is being laid on increasing original correspondence in Hindi in the Ministry of Defence. Progress made in this regard is reviewed regularly in the meetings of Official Language Implementation Committee headed by a Joint Secretary.

All notifications, service orders, service instructions, administrative reports and documents to be placed on the table of both the houses of parliament were prepared in bilingual form. Besides, papers for the cabinet and the consultative committee meetings were also prepared in both the languages.

ANNUAL PROGRAMME

Efforts were continued to be made this year also to achieve the targets laid down in the Annual Programme formulated by the Department of Official Language, Ministry of Home Affairs. A brief summary of the Annual Programme was prepared by the ministry and circulated to all officers and sections for compliance. The achievements made by them were reviewed quarterly in the meetings of Departmental Official Language Implementation Committees.

HINDI TRAINING

To impart training to the officers and staff of the ministry in Hindi, Hindi stenography and Hindi typing, nominations were continued to be made in batches during the year. The classes for such training are conducted by the Hindi Teaching Scheme of the Ministry of Home Affairs. The position relating to admissions actually taken by the nominees, their regular attendance in classes and taking examinations on the completion of the training was reviewed from time to time in quarterly Hindi meetings. Instructions by the ministry were issued to all defence organisations also to formulate a timebound programme for this purpose and ensure its implementation.

OFFICIAL LANGUAGE IMPLEMENTATION COMMITTEES

Two Hindi Advisory Committees have been constituted in the Ministry of Defence. Of these, one is meant for the Department of Defence and the other for the Department of Defence Production and Supplies and Defence Research and Development. The Defence Minister is the Chairman of both these Committees. After the expiry of three years' term, these committees are now being reconstituted. Similarly, there are two Official Language Implementation Committees functioning in this ministry with a view to review the official language implementation activities/achievements in the Ministry (main) and the three services headquarters, various inter-service organisations and defence undertakings and give useful suggestions to them. Four meetings of each of the two committees were held during the year at regular intervals of three months.

INCENTIVE SCHEMES

The Department of Official Language have formulated a number of incentive schemes to encourage the use of Hindi in the official work. All these schemes are already being run in the ministry and its attached and subordinate offices. These schemes include cash award scheme for noting and drafting in Hindi, special monthly allowance scheme for stenographers and typists for doing stenography and typing work in Hindi also in addition to English, cash award scheme for completing training in Hindi stenography and Hindi typing with distinctive marks, cash award scheme for officers giving maximum dictation in Hindi in addition to dictations in English, and so on.

All these schemes continued to be operative this year also. Two other schemes run by the Ministry of Defence with a view to encourage original writing in Hindi were also continued this year. Out of these schemes, one is meant for encouraging writing/translation of books in Hindi on various defence subjects. Under this biannual scheme, a provision of Rs. 40,000 and Rs. 12,000 has been made in the form of five and three cash prizes for the books written originally in Hindi and for those translated into Hindi.

Other scheme aims at encouraging the publication of good Hindi/bilingual in-house journals which are presently being brought out by more than 100 inter-service organisations, undertakings, offices, and so on. A large number of entries have been received this year under this scheme. Like previous years, it is proposed to give a total of Rs. 13,000/- by way of prizes to six magazines adjudged best in the order of merit.

INSPECTIONS

In order to ensure effective implementation of the annual

programme as also the orders /instructions of the Department of Official Language (Ministry of Home Affairs) regarding use of Hindi, a joint inspection team comprising officers from the Ministry of Defence, the Department of Official Language and the headquarters of the offices concerned, inspected 57 offices/ units located in different parts of the country during the year (up to November, 1998) under report. These inspections have proved helpful in creating appropriate conditions and awareness amongst the officers and employees for progressive use of Hindi in day-to-day official work.

MONITORING

The Ministry of Defence directly monitored the activities pertaining to implementation of the official language policy in the headquarters, of the various defence organisations. In the case of subordinate offices/units, this work was done through their headquarters.

During the year under report, this task was accomplished through official language inspections, review of their quarterly Hindi progress reports in the meetings of Official Language Implementation Committees of Ministry of Defence and also by attending the meetings of their Official Language Implementation Committees by the representatives of the Ministry of Defence. In addition to important suggestions given to these offices for removing their shortcomings, they were provided necessary guidance for achieving the targets laid down in the annual programme.

HINDI WORKSHOPS

To encouraging the officers/staff having proficiency/working knowledge of Hindi, to do their official work in Hindi as also to remove their hesitation arising out of lack of practice of working in Hindi, the Ministry of Defence organised three Hindi workshops in the year 1998-99 (up to November, 1998). Various defence organisations/offices located all over India also organised similar Hindi workshops which encouraged noting-drafting, originally in Hindi.

PURCHASE OF HINDI BOOKS

The Official Language Division has an important role to play in the meetings of Book Selection Committee of the Ministry of Defence which recommend Hindi/English books, magazines, and so on, for purchase by the Ministry of Defence, Inter-service organisations and the three service headquarters and so on. During the year 1998-99, these committees recommended 601 Hindi books.

HINDI FORTNIGHTS

A Hindi fortnight was organised in the Ministry as well as its various defence organisations with more jubilance and enthusiasm this year. In the ministry various Hindi competitions were held for motivating officers and staff to create an atmosphere of Hindi and thus increase its use in the day-to-day official work. The number of such competitions and that of the participants was more as compared to previous year.

With a view to encourage the participants and award them attractive prizes and so on an impressive prize distribution function was arranged in the ministry. The messages issued by the Home Minister, the Defence Minister and the Cabinet Secretary on this occasion were circulated/ read before officers and staff of the Ministry of Defence as well as its various organisations spread all over India.

SPECIAL SCHEMES/MEASURES

Hindi was resolved to be the official language of the Union by the Constituent Assembly on September 14, 1949. As such, this year happens to be the Golden Jubilee year of that historical event. In order to celebrate this occasion, some special measures are proposed to be taken this year to ensure progressive use of Hindi in the Ministry of Defence as well as its various organisations.

The ministry has decided to publish articles on subjects like modern aids, Indian language, freedom movement, progress of Hindi as well as on the lives of great men like Mahatma Gandhi, Netaji Subhash Chander Bose, and so on. in Hindi/ bilingual in-house magazines being brought out by various defence organisations this year. The ministry has issued necessary instructions in this regard to all defence organisations.

UN PEACEKEEPING OPERATIONS

India's first commitment to UN Peacekeeping efforts had arisen consequent to the war in Korea in 1950. Ever since, India has contributed military contingents, military observers and force commanders for UN peacekeeping forces all over the world.

Indian army contingents/observers remained deployed on UN peacekeeping operations in Angola, Sierra Leone, Kuwait and Lebanon, during the year. The professionalism and dedication of the Indian soldiers and the quality of their performance have been widely appreciated.

The respect for human rights displayed by Indian soldiers, often at risk to their own lives, has been recognised and respected by all nations. In terms of numbers today, India is the second highest contributor to UN peacekeeping operations. Indian troops currently posted as part of UN Military Mission Observer (MONUA) in Angola are not only involved in maintenence of peace but are also engaged in construction of quartering areas, reconstruction of bridges, reopening of roads, demining of roads as well as extending medical and humanitarian aid to the local populace.

In the UNOMSIL mission in Sierra Leone, the Indian Army has deployed a team of doctors and paramedics as part of the mission which itself is headed by an officer of the Indian Army. A team of 5 military observers from the Indian Army is deployed with the UN Observer Mission in Kuwait (UNIKOM) to monitor the sensitive demilitarised zone between Iraq and Kuwait. During 1998, a contingent of 617 personnel was deployed to Lebanon to replace the Norwegian contingent serving with the UNIFIL. The contingent is posted in a sensitive area near Golan Heights and their task involves domination of area of operation, prevention of infiltration/operations by local militias, protection of local population against attacks and provision of humanitarian aid. The induction of the Indian contingent has been welcomed by all other participants in UNIFIL as well as by the host country.

DEFENCE COOPERATION WITH FOREIGN COUNTRIES

The enhancement and strengthening of defence cooperation

with foreign countries continued to be an important objective and component of our overall defence and foreign policy. Consequent upon the significant changes that have taken place in recent years in the global political and strategic environment, and even as our traditional defence ties have been maintained, defence-related cooperation with a large number of countries has been progressed.

The fifth session of the Indo-Russian Group on Military-Technical cooperation was held in Moscow from November 10 to 12, 1998. The meetings of the Joint Indo-Russian Group on Military-Technical Cooperation, held in New Delhi and Moscow, have been constructive and fruitful and have enabled not only the structuring of the content of cooperation in the form of a long-term programme of cooperation up to the year 2000 and beyond, but have also afforded an opportunity for high level and functional review, to resolve impediments to the successful implementation of the programme.

During the visit of Russian Prime Minister to India from December 20-22, 1998, an agreement on long-term programme of military-technical cooperation between India and Russia up to the year 2010 was signed. The first meeting of the Indo-French High Committee on Defence Cooperation was held in Paris from May 4 to 6, 1998. This committee supersedes the Joint Working Committee on Defence Cooperation set up under the provisions of the Memorandum of Understanding on Defence Cooperation between the two countries signed in 1982.

During the meeting, both sides declared their intention to give a new impetus to the development of bilateral defence relations and agreed that Indo-French cooperation should be based on a long term perspective and corresponding commitments in defence research and development, defence industry and relations between the armed forces of the two countries.

This cooperation is part of the overall Indo-French relationship and must be based on an understanding and appreciation of each other's vital and strategic security interests and aspirations. The first meeting of Indo-South

African joint Committee on Defence Cooperation was held in Pretoria in August 1998. The Defence Secretary headed the Indian delegation for this meeting. During the meeting it was agreed that progress in the defence sector was a concrete manifestation of the desires of India and South Africa to build a strategic partnership between the two countries.

Views were exchanged on the security environment in their respective regions and on issues and developments that affect regional security and stability. The second Indo-Italian joint Committee meeting that was scheduled to be held in the first week of November 1998 has been postponed for the year 1999.

A high level delegation led by Minister of National Defence of the Hellenic Republic visited India during December 5-9, 1998. A Memorandum of Understanding on defence cooperation between India and Greece was signed during the visit. The defence cooperation meetings, and other high level interactions with other countries, provided an opportunity to review the structure and content of defence cooperation with a view to further strengthening them. The Defence Ministers of Kyrgyz and Maldives visited India during February 1999 and the Defence Minister of Russian Federation and Romania visited India in March 1999.

After India conducted nuclear tests on May 11 and 13, 1998, the Governments of Australia, United States of America, United Kingdom and Japan reacted very adversely. This has resulted in closing of our defence ties with these countries. Subsequently, the visits of Chief of Army Staff and Chief of Naval Staff to UK were cancelled.

Cooperation with the constituent States of the Association of South East Nations (ASEAN) and the ASEAN Regional Forum (ARF) continued through the period. The Indian delegation participated at the various Inter-Sessional Group (ISG) meetings held on subjects such as Peace-Keeping Operations, Confidence Building Measures (CBMs), Disaster Management, Search and Rescue (SAR), International Security, Politics and Economics, and Production of Defence Policy Documents. We attach great significance. To exchange of visits at the level of service chiefs is an important measure for promoting goodwill between our armed forces and their foreign counterparts. During the period under review, the Chief of Army Staff (COAS) visited South-Africa and Syria. The Chief of Air Staff (CAS) visited Chile, the Chief of Naval Staff (CNS) visited Russia and Bangladesh and the Vice Chief of Army Staff visited Tanzania.

16

Departments of the Ministry of Defence

Department of Defence

1. Department of Defence of India and every part thereof including preparation for defence and all such acts as may be conducive in times of war to its prosecution and, after its termination, to effective demobilisation.
2. The Armed Forces of the Union, namely, the Army, the Navy, the Air Force.
3. The Reserves of the Army, Navy and Air Force.
4. Territorial Army.
5. The National Cadet Corps.
6. Works relating to Army, Navy, Air Force and Ordnance Factories.
7. Remounts, Veterinary and Farms Organisation.
8. Canteen Stores Department (India).
9. Civilian Services paid from Defence Estimates.
10. Hydrographic Surveys and preparation of navigational charts.
11. Formation of Cantonments, delimitation/excision of Cantonment areas, local self-government in such areas, the constitution and powers within such areas of Cantonment Boards authorities and the regulation of house accommodation (including the control of rents) in such areas.

12. Acquisition, requisitioning, custody and relinquishment of land and property for defence purposes. Eviction of unauthorised occupants from defence land and property.
13. Matters relating to ex-Servicemen including Pensioners.
14. Defence Accounts Department.
15. Purchase of foodstuffs for military requirements and their disposal excluding those entrusted to Ministry of Food and Civil Supplies (Department of Food).
16. Coast Guard Organisation.
17. Matters relating to diving and related activities in the country.
18. The following Inter-Service Organisations function under the Ministry of Defence:
    i) Office of the Chief Administrative Officer.
    ii) Armed Forces Medical Services.
    iii) National Defence College.
    iv) Directorate of Public Relations.
    v) Armed Forces Film and Photo Division.
    vi) School of Foreign Languages.
    vii) Historical Section.
    viii) Directorate General Defence Estates.
    ix) Services Sports Control Board.
    x) College of Defence Management, Secunderabad.
    xi) Ministry of Defence Library.

DEPARTMENT OF DEFENCE PRODUCTION AND SUPPLIES

19. Ordnance Factory Board and Ordnance Factories.
20. Hindustan Aeronautics Limited (HAL).
21. Bharat Electronics Limited (BEL).
22. Mazagon Docks Limited (MDL).

23. Garden Reach Shipbuilders and Engineers Limited (GRSE).

24. Goa Shipyard Limited (GSL).

25. Bharat Dynamics Limited (BDL).

26. Mishra Dhatu Nigam Limited (MIDHANI).

27. Directorate General of Quality Assurance (DGQA) including Directorate of Technical Development and Production (Air).

28. Standardisation of defence equipments and stores including Directorate of Standardisation.

29. Bharat Earth Movers Limited (BEML).

30. Development of aeronautics industry and coordination among users other than those concerned with the Department of Civil Aviation and the Department of Space.

31. Indigenisation, development and production of items required for defence purposes.

32. Procurement exclusive to the defence services.

DEPARTMENT OF DEFENCE RESEARCH AND DEVELOPMENT

33. Apprising, assessing and advising the Defence Minister on the influence on national security of emerging developments in science and technology.

34. Rendering advice to the Defence Minister and to the three services and inter-services organisations on all scientific aspects of weapons; weapon platforms; military operations; surveillance; support and logistics, in all likely theatres of conflict.

35. To function, with the concurrence of the Ministry of External Affairs, as the nodal coordinating agency of the Ministry of Defence on all matters relating to instruments of accord with foreign governments relating to the acquisition of technologies whose export to India is the subject of national security-related controls of foreign governments.

36. Formulation and execution of programmes of scientific research and design, development, test and evaluation, in fields of relevance to national security.

37. Direction and administration agencies, laboratories, establishments, ranges, facilities, programmes and projects of the department.

38. Aeronautical Development Agency.

39. All matters relating to certification of the design, air-worthiness of military aircraft, their equipment and stores.

40. All matters relating to the protection and transfer of technology generated by the activities of the department.

41. Scientific analysis, support and participation in acquisition and evaluation proceedings of all weapon systems and related technologies proposed to be acquired by the Ministry of Defence.

42. To render advice on the technological and intellectual property aspects of the import of technology by production units and enterprises manufacturing, or proposing to manufacture, equipment and stores for the armed services.

43. To deal with reference made under section 35 of the Patents Act, 1970 (39 of 1970).

44. Financial and other material assistance to individuals, institutions and bodies corporate, for study and for the training of manpower on aspects of science and Technology that bear on national security.

45. In consultation with the Ministry of External Affairs, on international relations in matters connected with the role of science and technology in national security including:

    i) Matters relating to relations with research organisations of other countries and with inter-governmental agencies, particularly those which concern themselves, inter alia, with the scientific and technological aspects of national security.

ii) Arrangement with universities, educational and research-oriented institutions or bodies corporate abroad to provide fore foreign scholarships and the training of Indian scientists and technologists under the administrative control of the department.

46. Execution of works and purchase of lands debitable to the budget of the department.

47. All matters relating to personnel under the control of the department.

48. Acquisition of all types of stores, equipment and services debitable to the budget of the department.

49. Any other activity assigned to, accepted by, the Department through understanding or arrangements with any other ministry, department, agency of the Government of India whose activities have a bearing on the scientific and technological aspect of national security.

DEFENCE (FINANCE) DIVISION

50. To examine all defence matters having a financial bearing.

51. To render financial advice to the various functionaries of Ministry of Defence and the service headquarters.

52. To act as integrated finance Division of the Ministry of Defence.

53. To assist in the formulation and implementation of all schemes/proposals involving expenditure.

54. To assist in the formulation and implementation of defence plans.

55. To prepare the defence budget and other estimates for the defence services and to monitor the progress of the schemes against the budget.

56. To exercise post-budget vigilance to ensure that there are neither considerable shortfalls in expenditure nor unforeseen excesses.

57. To advise heads of branches of the armed forces headquarters in the discharge of their financial responsibility.

58. To function as the accounting authority for the defence Services.

59. To prepare the appropriation accounts for the defence services.

60. To discharge the responsibility for payments and internal audit of defence expenditure through the Controller General of Defence Accounts.

Index